LIVING YOUR BEST LIFE

DISCOVER PRACTICAL WAYS TO:

STRETCH YOUR PAYCHECK

SAVE YOUR MONEY

VACATION

AND MUCH MORE

D Wayne Shearer

DEDICATION

First to God Almighty, to whom I owe my life. To my loving, faithful wife and partner of 29 years (I Love Us) – thank you. To my son, full of talent and passion, you are purposed for the kingdom of God. To my daughter and her husband, they are my most favorite couple. To my grandsons, they keep me motivated. Thank you all for your love, respect and support.

CONTENTS

INTRODUCTION

I'm sure you've realized by now that survival without finances is not an option. Listen to the conversations around you, there are too many families whose finances are out of control and as a result they are in financial bondage. This means that people are all too familiar with over the limit credit cards, department store accounts, car loans, student loans, as well as gambling, bingo, over spending, impulse purchasing and making uncertain financial investments. Whichever it may be, these money drains have no promising financial growth for your household income or your future. Though many of these items appear to be the right answer to becoming financially stable, unfortunately, you later find out that they are crutches which fast become the master of your finances. These monetary devices can cause an unhealthy relationship between you and your finances, which adds unnecessary stress (and who needs that?).

The question now is, how do you release yourself from being bound to these services? Well, stop the worrying; I know it appears virtually impossible to relieve yourself from this downward spiral towards a financial disaster. But, the good news is the chains of debt enslavement can be broken! YOU have a choice! The scriptures declare, "I can do all things through Christ who strengthens me!"

While we are quoting the Bible let's remember Proverbs 3:15 that says, "in all your getting get understanding". As we journey through the three sections of this book you will see that obtaining financial control and being rid of debt requires implementing principles set by the Lord Himself. You may be familiar with many of the principles and standards we use, because they have been around since the beginning of time. We'll also refer to many philosophical entries and practical living tips established and written in the good book (The Bible) for our benefit. We have studied the promises, the principles and practical living tips concerning financial growth. Now after praying for wisdom and practicing these things in our own lives, we are blessed to bring it all together in one place that it may be a blessing and a benefit to you.

As you read this book coupled with your faith, your wisdom and your consistent application of these practical living tips to your everyday life, success is eminent. We believe you will learn to maximize your present income, minimize your debt, and become a better steward over what God has blessed you with, positioning yourself for greater things. Ready? Let's get it!!!

SECTION 1

"Having What It Takes"

First you must know that God created man (woman) in his image and in _His likeness_ (Genesis 1:27). This basically means that the Lord has imparted in you everything you need to succeed, to overcome and to have victory. After creating man (woman), He told them be fruitful, multiply, replenish and subdue in the earth (Genesis 1:28). This refers to everything on the earth, including your finances.

Think about this: when God created the earth, He furnished it with trees, plants, animals, water, blue skies, wind and light. Everything man-kind needed was imparted in the earth. He put man into this creation and told him to subdue it and have dominion over it. We did. Take notice of the liberties we enjoy today; we use trees for products that range from writing paper to luxurious mansions. Out of the ground we produce minerals, oils, medicines, precious stones etc. and don't forget the food, the clothing, the cars and entertainment. Everything we enjoy was already here. We must remember to tap into what God has imparted in us to succeed, we are made in His likeness.

> **Deuteronomy 8:18 (NIV) says:** _"But remember the Lord your God, for it is He who gives you the ability to produce wealth, and so confirms His covenant, which He swore to your ancestors, as it is today."_

So, what I'm saying is; you can do it. Yes, you can! Yes, you can create a budget and follow it. Yes, you can minimize your debt. Yes, you can eliminate your debt. Yes, you can have financial control! The ability has already been put in you. What needs to happen now is you have to wrap your mind around this truth. Listen, if you will change the way you think, you can change your future.

Romans 12:2 says:
"be transformed by the renewing of your mind"

Yes, believe it, you can handle your financial situation, so arm yourself with the information needed to accomplish this task. (you have started well, by reading this book)

Luke 12:48 (NKJV) says:
"To whom much is given, from them much is required"

Hey, don't be intimidated. Do what you already know to do, but don't stop there. Francis Bacon (1597) said, "knowledge is power". Get all you can get. The bible says in Proverbs 3, "lean not to your own understanding but in all your ways acknowledge the Lord and He will direct your paths and blessed is the one who finds wisdom and obtains understanding. So, in all you're getting, get understanding. "

Deuteronomy 8:18 (NIV) says:
"He gives us the ability to get wealth"

We have to work (start) with what we've already been given.

Having what it takes to be successful is essential to having success. Be sure to read books, take classes, attend seminars and ask lots of questions pertaining to financial literacy including but not limited to budgeting, saving, investing and retirement.

BEING A GOOD STEWARD

A steward: one who has been entrusted to handle the business and the affairs of another, highly regarded as responsible, dependable, responsible (yes I said it again. *it bears repeating; it is your responsibility to be responsible*), able and trustworthy. Sounds like I'm talking about you.

A steward is also defined as a fiduciary: One who prudently takes care of money for another. Yes it all belongs to Him but He has entrusted you to call it your own, enjoy it and handle it wisely.

There is a great responsibility and expectation that comes along with getting this blessing.

It has been proven, *"Whoever can be trusted with very little, can also be trusted with much and whoever is dishonest with very little will also be dishonest with much. If you haven't been trustworthy in handling someone else's property, who will give you your own?" (Luke16:10,12)(NIV).* Well, it's exciting to know that the BIG GUY (The Lord, Almighty) considers us trustworthy.

This position requires of us to be good stewards (managers) over our finances and recognizing the value of money will perfect our efforts in managing it.

People seek money because it has purchasing power. With money we enjoy life's necessities, life's luxuries and entertainment. The purchasing power of money is determined by the demand for money and the supply of money, like the prices we pay for the products and services we use. Money is used as a medium of exchange. Our demands for money may be influenced by consideration of facts and circumstances associated with the products or services we enjoy. Let me explain...............

With the Products

The short version says supply and demand can greatly affect the value of the dollar. When the demand for products and services are high and the supply is low, then prices tend to increase (stuff is expensive). In contrast, the greater the supply and the lower the demand the prices tend to fall (stuff goes on sale). Some economists say the level of taxation is an important factor in determining the exchange value of money. A recent article read that oppressive tax burdens causes goods prices to rise and the purchasing power of money to fall. Thanks to the entrepreneurs and capitalists of this country we've been blessed to keep a balance of capital and goods as to avoid a deep recession over the past several years.

In layman's terms it translates into: don't let '*I want more*' manage your finances because if you do, '*I need more*' will be broke. It's been my experience, that if you do what you *need* to do, then maybe, you may have enough left over to do what you *want* to do (your purchasing power will strengthen if you do what you need to do first).

It's time to grind; a man must work
"The one who is unwilling to work shall not eat"
2 Thessalonians 3:10 (NIV)

With the Money

There are several factors that could affect the demand for money, such as inflation, uncertainty about the future and interest rates. Another factor that affects the demand for money, is having a growing population with individuals earning money and establishing cash holdings that may generate new demand which could raise the purchasing power of money and reduce the prices of goods.

In layman's terms: having more cash makes you a game changer, it gives you more "say so" and more control over your finances and your future.

Money answers all things
"Festivals are for laughter, wine makes life pleasant,
and money speaks to everything"
Ecclesiastes 10:19 (ISV)

You want to change your life? Change the way you think
Romans 12:2 (AMP) says *"And do not be conformed to this world [any longer with its superficial values and customs], but be* [a] *transformed and progressively changed [as you mature spiritually] by the renewing of your mind [focusing on godly values and ethical attitudes], so that you may prove [for yourselves] what the will of God is, that which is good and acceptable and perfect [in His plan and purpose for you].*

Educating yourself about the value of money and understanding your earning potential are necessary steps to securing a healthy financial future. Your family's current household income can give you a glimpse into what your retirement may look like. Take a gander at the chart below and see how your current earnings will empower you in the coming years.

These earning potential numbers in chart 1-1 don't take into account any raises or other changes to your income. For an opportunity to have a more secure financial portfolio, explore income diversity, which is having multiple streams of income. See Chart 1-2 on the next page.

Number of Years Saving	YOUR YEARLY EARNING POTENTIAL			
	$30,000	$50,000	$100,000	$250,000
3	$90,000	$150,000	$300,000	$750,000
5	$150,000	$250,000	$500,000	$1,250,000
10	$300,000	$500,000	$1,000,000	$2,500,000
15	$450,000	$750,000	$1,500,000	$3,750,000
20	$500,000	$1,000,000	$2,000,000	$5,000,000
25	$750,000	$1,250,000	$2,500,000	$6,250,000
30	$900,000	$1,500,000	$3,000,000	$7,500,000
35	$1,050,000	$1,750,000	$3,500,000	$8,750,000
40	$1,200,000	$2,000,000	$4,000,000	$10,000,000

Chart 1-1

My Assets

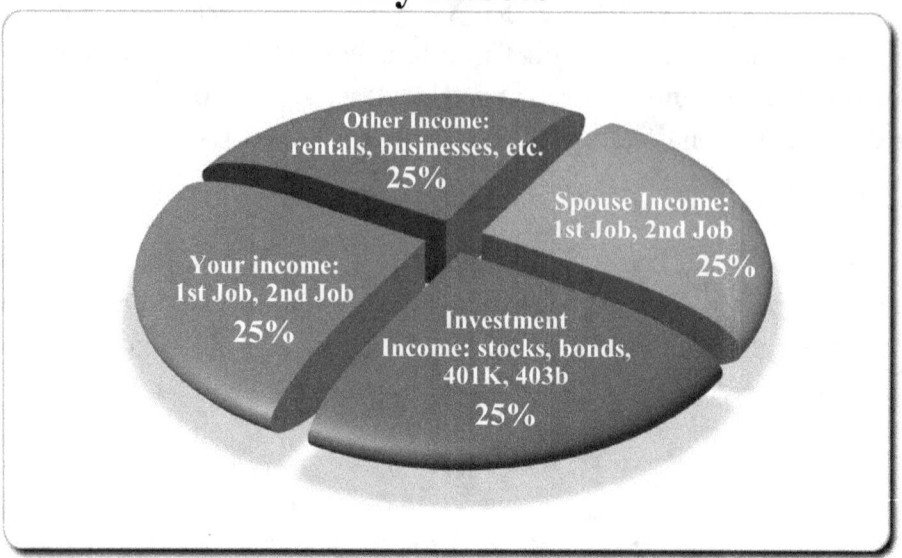

Chart1-2

The numbers in the chart 1-1 are encouraging, right? The challenge here is to restructure your finances and develop a plan that allows you to keep most of the income you receive. This restructuring must include a savings plan and an investment strategy for the recovered earnings in order to make these projections a reality. I believe you must take a personal inventory of your spending habits and then identify the transactions that adversely affect your cash. You should also make a list of things in your life which may be important to you and could affect your financial future; items such as family, health, lifestyle, retirement, work, education, etc. These items should be categorized and prioritized as they will be a key component in how you restructure and plan for maximizing your income.

You will find tools in the next section that will assist you in your restructuring journey.

Plan It or Forget It

Take time and begin planning your future. Setting standards for yourself will help in eliminating your current financial debt. You must have a vision for your future *(take part in writing your own story, you are the right person for the task, you have the power!)*. Your vision should encompass every area of your life. With a vision your destination is more apparent and taking time to write it down makes it more realistic. You have to *plan it* or you'll *forget it.*

Winston Churchill said: *"He who fails to plan is planning to fail"*

Habakkuk 2:2 (AMP) says
"Write the vision and make it plain on tablets, So that the one who reads it will run. For the vision is yet for the future time, it hurries toward the goal of fulfillment; it will not fail."

Here are some (game changer) exercises that will assist you in bringing your vision together:

1. Values List

2. Dream List

3. Goal List

4. Career List

5. Education List

6. No Limit List

7. Travel Goals List

8. Financial Goals List

9. Need To Do List

Please be sure to include your spouse in these (game changer) exercises as it will make the difference in restructuring your entire household finances.

Values List

Values are considered to be morals that are important to you. The values list will help you notice specific characteristics about yourself and your spouse. When completing this exercise, it is imperative to be open and honest with yourself. Another factor to consider; plainly stated, don't be critical of your spouse's list!! You may notice similarities as well as dissimilar values. This exercise can open the door for healthy discussion and growth. Sensitivity and kindness goes a long way.

VALUES LIST

What's important to you?
"For as a man thinks in his heart, so he is"
Proverbs 23:7

√ Which are important	Prioritize: 1st, 2nd, 3rd, etc.	
_____	_____	Happiness
_____	_____	More free time
_____	_____	a close relationship w/God
_____	_____	family (spending more time)
		peace of mind

Dreams List

You are free to dream. Dreaming is an expression of freedom, it relieves stress, builds morale, and stimulates your joy, which gives you strength. Dreaming is in-order and a must have. This ability to imagine leads to wonderful accomplishments and overflowing blessings (especially when you're trusting God). So, be free and enjoy the blessings of the Lord.

Dreaming exemplifies the promise of the Lord…
"…all things are possible through Christ who strengthens me"
Philippians 4:13 (NKJV)

DREAMS LIST

My Dream

1. Mercedes C30 _____

2. _____

Spouse's Dream

1. New Kitchen Cabinets ____ .

2. _____

DREAMS LIST

Now you try. Remember this, there are no boundaries here. No dream is too big and there are no insignificant dreams either. God is the limit. Have fun!

My Dream

1. _____

2. _____

3. _____

Spouse's Dream

1. _____

2. _____

3. _____

GOAL LIST

Goals are necessary in realizing your vision. Consider them to be road signs to your destiny. Use your goals as encouragement to keep you focused. <u>Do not</u> limit your goals to budgeting, we believe you should set and accomplish goals to the highest extent you <u>desire</u>. Taking the limits off will help you maximize your ability that God has given you and cause you to see your vision clearly and achieve your destiny. Be sure to set short-term goals for momentum (1 -3years) intermediate goals for reminders to stay the course (3-10 years) and long term-goals for security and stability (10 years or more).

"Goals are directions to your dreams"

(know this one thing…"He Is Able to [carry out His purpose and] do superabundantly more than all that we dare ask or think [infinitely beyond our greatest prayers, hopes, or dreams], according to His power that is at work in us"…)
Ephesians 3:20 AMP

GOALS LIST

Short-Term Goals (1-3 years)	How?	Start Date	Accomplish Date
Start saving $25.00 per pay / no eating out			
Lose 2 lbs per week / no sweets, more walking			
Paint the kitchen this weekend / wake up at 5am sat morning			
Write in my journal every day for 5 min. /during my lunch time			
Pay $25.00 extra towards principle on car loan /do my own nails			

Mid-Term Goals (4-9 years)	How	Start Date	Accomplish Date
Save $2,500.00 yearly /			
Maintain a healthy diet /			
Paint every room of the house /			

Short-term goals are often the vehicle for long-term goals. *("Delight yourself in the Lord and He shall give you the desires of your heart") psalms 37:4 (NKJV)*

CAREER GOALS

Personal accomplishments give us gratification, it builds self-esteem and enables us to share and be a blessing to others. Complete the following four exercises in the activities section of your workbook, so that you can determine the path of success you are traveling.......

CAREER GOALS LIST

"Be all you can be, God is the Limit"

Where do you currently work? What is your position?

_____

Current hourly rate $_____ Current annual salary $_____
one year formula for a 40 hour a week job: 2080(hours) x $ (hourly rate) = annual income

Is there room for growth at this company? Available promotions:

Right Now 1) _____   salary $_____

In 1 year   2) _____   salary $_____

in 5 years   3) _____   salary $_____

in 10 year   4. _____   salary $_____

Are You ready for change?

EDUCATIONAL GOALS

Any plan worth executing is worth writing down. Whatever you may need, write it down, whatever you may want , write it down. Set no limits to your master mind. Each goal set is reachable with the strength and faith you possess. Set it and accomplish it. Who says you can't?!

EDUCATIONAL GOALS LIST

"with all your getting, get understanding" proverbs 4:7

Name of conference/ course/class & college	Start Date	Finish Date	Cost $
1. _____	_____	_____	_____
Purpose: _____			
2. _____	_____	_____	_____
Purpose: _____			
3. _____			
Purpose: _____			

No Limit List

Having Dreams and Settings goals should be fun, so turn your dreams into goals and have fun. This list is to cover any list we didn't cover (some of these items you may have listed on other lists and that's ok, the only rule here is, Go For It!!!)

tip: psalms 37:4

NO LIMITS LIST

"I can do all things through Christ who strengthens me"
Philippians 4:13

Your Desire   Goal Date

1. _____   _____

2. _____   _____

3. _____

TRAVEL GOALS

For me, traveling clears my mind of stuff. Here I get in touch with peace, joy and the inner me. It's truly soothing and invigorating; allowing me to return with a fresh perspective and a new attitude.

(GO AND EXPLORE THE WORLD THAT THE LORD HAS MADE)

TRAVEL GOALS LIST

(GO AND EXPLORE THE WORLD THAT THE LORD HAS MADE)

"The earth is the Lord's and everything in it, the world and all who live in it."
Psalm 24:1 NIV

State-side Destinations	Cost	Goal Date
1.		
2.		
3.		
4.		
5.		

International Destination (Overseas)	Cost	Goal Date
1.		

FINANCIAL GOALS

It's your money, make it work for you. Are you up for the challenge?......Lets Go!!!

FINANCIAL GOALS LIST

The challenge is not how much you make.
It's how much you can keep.

Category	Present	1 Year	5 year	10 Year	Retirement
401K	$3000.00	$10,000.00	$56,000.00	$104,000.00	$253,000.00
Savings Acct.	$1,200.00	$2500.00	$6,000.00		
Investments	N/A				

How will I make this Happen

"BE INTENTIONAL.....NEVER FAILING"

1. Take an investment class

2. Read books on budgeting

3. Open an investment

There is a budgeting chart in the next section! (full blank forms are in the workbook) (SOLD SEPERATELY)

23

NEED TO DO LIST

I love these List. They have changed my life. They have helped me take the limits off and now, I realize that I can do anything through Christ, who has blessed me.

-Get a list, write it down, make it plain...this is the season, today is

NEED TO DO LIST

"If you Do what you need to do when you need to do it, then the day will come when you can do what you want to do when you want to do it."
— Zig Ziglar

Get-er Done List

item	start date	finish date
1. _____	_____	_____
2. _____	_____	_____
3. _____	_____	_____
4. _____	_____	_____
5. _____		
6. _____		
7. _____		

SECTION 2

"Getting Organized"

Filing For Success

It's hard to know what's going on in your financial life when things are here, there and everywhere. Wouldn't you like to be less stressed? Wouldn't you like to have more time on your hands? Would you also like to be organized? If your answer is yes to these questions, let's do this: take control of your finances and your future. I believe success starts with a dream and there are two types of dreamers; individuals who accomplish their dreams and those who only hope to accomplish their dreams, the difference between them is "control". Being organized can reduce stress, save you time, give you the professional look and put you in control all at the same time. Are you ready for a fresh Start? Great.

FIRST - collect all important papers and financial documents to begin the process of "filing for success". This includes all of your creditors (mortgages, credit cards, vehicle loans, etc.). Now gather invoices for your monthly living expenses (gas & electric, water works, phone bill, etc.). You'll want to gather statements for your financial institutions, i.e., banks/credit union's (checking accounts, savings account, 401k accounts, 403b, and any money market accounts). We have included a worksheet (there's a sample below), on it list all of your creditors and living expenses in the appropriate section. After you have completed that task, put the invoices and statements aside for now in separate stacks. We will come back to them shortly.

SECOND - here's a list of some items needed to create your own personal and professional home office:

* Two drawer filing cabinet
* Hanging folders with labels
* Two bins (labeled in/out)
* Paper shredder
* small desk/table (with a comfortable chair)
* computer/laptop (a refurbished unit will be fine for personal business use)

* pens/pencils/paper clips
* scissors/white out/copy paper
* all-in-one copy/fax/scanner/printer
* if the budget allows: internet
* calculator

Find an area in your home where you can comfortably set up these items. It could be a corner of any room or the spare bedroom. Once you have these items in place, go ahead and make your new office cozy-add a picture and maybe a small plant.

THIRD - We are living in a time where technology has simplified our organizing process. So upload and utilize the charts we provide to help you organize your personal business and keep track of your important transactions. You should also take advantage of scanning all important documents, saving them to your computer and as well as to a flash drive. Store the flash drive in a safe place. We also recommend that you file a hard copy of all important documents in a safe place that you can quickly access.

Now grab the stack of papers of all your creditors, bank accounts, investment accounts etc., also grab the new folders and labels. Label a file folder for each of the creditors and expenses you have. You will also want to create a file and label for other personal information such as wills, insurance policies, educational information, passwords, equipment warranties, birth certificates, medical records, etc.). Hey listen, it is ok to make a file for everything you have going on in your life. Being organized gives you more control. Over do it if you need to, until you develop good organizational habits. After completing this task, put the folders in alphabetical order and place them in your new file cabinet.

Congratulations, not only have you just created your own "personal office", now your personal and financial information are all at your fingertips. These steps will assist you and your family in the management, distribution, and the future planning of your finances.

Along with the new filing system we have developed some steps for you to follow, in order to stay on the right path. So, kick off your shoes or not! Relax! And let's figure some things out!

KNOWING WHAT'S COMING AND GOING

You could be wealthy already. Maybe you've paid off your car loan. Maybe you sent 2 payments to the bill collector. Well, you'll never know until you track all the money that's coming in and the money that's going out. You must be aware of how much money you and your spouse bring home each month. With the same enthusiasm you must know what's going out. Here's what you can do: collect a month worth of pay stubs from everyone that contributes to the household income. You will then look for the net and gross amounts on each stub. Calculate separately the net and

27

gross amounts from each of the stubs for the entire month you saved your stubs. The totals will be your monthly income with the net being what you actually bring home. In like manner keep a record of all spending done by the money earners in the house. This means keep all check stubs from bill payments, all receipts and you can also write down over the phone credit card transactions and every purchase made during this month including honey buns, soda pop, potato chips, manicures and haircuts. Categorize the canceled checks and receipts into groups such as food, entertainment, auto, stress spending (lol), etc.. now total the amount of all the spending.

Example:

1. It is a good practice to know where your money is going, starting with how you go from gross to net. Gross pay is the amount of money you make before deductions; these deduction may include federal taxes, state and local taxes, social security tax, and Medicare tax. You may also elect to have retirement contributions come out of your gross pay, as well as vacation and Christmas account contributions. After all these deductions are distributed, you then receive the balance of your earning known as your pay check/net pay.

2. Now make an entry for each creditor (bill) you owe. Follow the worksheet to determine your total expense for a month.

3. Remember to always keep a record of your creditors, the amount owed, the due date (not the late date) and the interest rate if applicable.

The Leftovers

Most people think of leftovers as a fantastic bounty, but there are many who refuse leftovers and view them as a moralistic chore. I Do NOT prefer leftover food, but I do appreciate leftover money. With that said, having leftover food paves the way for saving money (leftover money). So let's practice acquiring a taste for leftovers.

After the exercise above you should have two totals: an amount of what you have coming in and an amount of what's going out. Using your new calculator subtract going\$ from coming\$ (coming\$ – going\$ = what's leftover). Ok, what do you have??? = 0...hey there's still hope. Now you're getting the motivation to bring about a change.. or (some change$).   Whichever make *"cents."*

Example: $2500 (income) - $2275 (expenses) = $225 leftover

TRACK'N THE CHANGE

While it is important to track the creditors and the expenses that are being paid. It is as equally important to track all other monetary spending. This includes whatever you spend your hard earned money on: groceries, gas, household products, extra-curricular activities, restaurants, gift giving, coffee stops, honey buns, chewing gum, etc. I have created a worksheet for you to "track the change", use it to record every cent that is spent.   A habit I developed is to get and keep all receipts from every purchase made and at the end of each day I consult with my spouse to see what receipts she may have and we would record this information on the worksheet. Seeing is believing and when you believe, you can make a difference, so write the information on the worksheet. Adopting this method or something similar to it, will make it easier for you to track your spending and tracking your change won't require a GPS.

TRACKING THE CHANGE

DATE	ITEM /STORE	AMOUNT
_____	_____	$_____
_____	_____	$_____
_____	_____	$_____

SAVING THE CHANGE

After you GPS where your change is going, now you may want to think about how you can cut cost and start saving some change. Here are a few suggestions that can jump start your cost cutting and ultimately power-down your bills.

- Organize your travel time to save gas
- Pack lunch more times during the week
- Eliminate your snacks between home and work.

Penny Pinching
Tips to reduce expense and produce some cents

(be sure to record your current bill amount before the changes, then monitor the savings)

1. Household:

- Take advantage of federal tax credits for energy efficiency with Energy Star (look up online)
- Winter time. Turn thermostat down a few degrees at night and layer on the pajamas.
- Install a programmable thermostat (and use it)
- Put insulating wrap on hot water tank
- Insulate all exposed hot water lines
- Use high efficiency LED bulbs
- Unplug electrical items when not in use (they are vampire items that suck electricity when they are not in use, such as cell phone plugs, flat irons, toasters, Xboxes, etc.
- Turn off the lights, please. (when not in use)
- Use the sun to help heat the house during the winter time
- Close the blinds on hot days during the summer time
- Fix or replace the drippy faucet
- Make sure the toilet water isn't running (if your water is clear, sprinkle a little kool-aid powder in the tank, don't flush. If there is a slow leak, in about 5 minutes you will see the kool-aid color in your toilet bowl. If so, it is time to replace the guts in the tank. Your local hardware store will have what you need. Be sure to get water efficient replacements.
- Spring clean the house and have a yard sale (great way to help power-down a bill or even fund a planned vacation)
- Insulate your home and use fans and ventilation instead of AC
- Do routine maintenance on your household items
- Down size (house, vehicle, entertainment, etc.)
- Try basic cable or a local channel antenna

2. At the Store

- Clip coupons (for all your shopping- grocery, clothing, entertainment, etc. there are several coupon free apps available to help you save money with some of your expenses)
- Buy in bulk and get rewards cards at the supermarket.
- Always Ask for a discount on large purchases like appliances or electronics.
- Don't follow your impulse. If you feel the urge to buy something, wait. There is a 30 day wait rule if you're disciplined. Or at least wait a few days and see if you still want it or need it (do what u need to do 1st).
- Wait for sales
- Plan your meals for the week
- Make a grocery list and stick to it.
- At the grocery store look down. Items below eye level are often cheaper.
- Buy generic (ingredients are generally the same)
- If you cannot afford food, find a food bank that gives out bags of groceries.
- Shop for holiday gifts after the holiday

3. Save money on gas:

- (keep oil changed regularly, keep a clean air filter and maintain correct air pressure in tires, these things help conserve your gas)
- Car pool when possible (ride to church together ☺)
- Plan your driving errands and trips
- Walk or ride your bike or take the bus

4. Save Money Everywhere:

- Keep a budget and analyze every expense that you make.
- Shop car insurance get at least 3 quotes
- Raise your car insurance deductible for a lower monthly

payment (if you're a good driver)

- Buy used, shop craigslist first
- You can raise your deductible for home owner's insurance for a lower quote
- Make sure that you have health insurance. (www.healthcare.gov, may be a good place to start and compare premiums)
- Get a mortgage refinance quote to see if you pay too much for home payments.
- Travel cheap. Stay at <u>Hostels</u>, <u>Couch Surf</u> or <u>Air BnB.</u>
- Pack lunch and bring coffee (scratch the coffee shop)
- Cancel that unused membership (gym, music apps, annual fee memberships, etc.)
- Get a credit report at <u>AnnualCreditReport.com</u>, the government sponsored credit reporting website.
- Make gifts instead of purchasing
- For entertainment: the library has plenty of books, CD's and DVDs. You can also request that the library buy certain books.
- Empty your pockets at night; put all change in the piggy bank (dollars and coins, it adds up).
- Take up hobbies that don't cost money.
- Quit smoking and save: check this out: <u>$8 each</u> X <u>2 packs -a-day</u> X <u>5 years</u> @ <u>.03% interest</u> = $29,238 (that .03% is with a regular savings account, investment accounts yield more).
- Buy a quality used car instead of new (purchase an extended warranty with it)
- Switch to term life insurance
- Follow your budget
- Watch out for Fees. Fees are everywhere; bank fees, atm fees, cash checking fees, late fees. These can add up over time. (know the requirements and monitor your statements)
- some banks offer incentives and perks for new accounts.

Check out the local banks and the online banks as well.

- Cook a meal; save a great deal of money (and you'll have leftovers)
- Eat breakfast at home
- use auto bill pay to avoid late fees (your bank has to be online and make sure the money is in your account)

Now that you are mastering cutting cost and keeping track of your savings, it's time to benefit from the proceeds. Looking back at "Track'n the Change", recall the excess amount and the amount you saved from cost of living cutting...add them together. For example:

Let's say in your list you noticed that you spend $2.00 a day, everyday after work; assuming you work 5 days a week, that adds up to $40.00 a month. ($2 x 5 Days a week x 4 weeks). So, that's a $40.00 cut (net) from your list. And assume you cut cost by $30.00 using coupons on your grocery bill. So getting rid of a $40 habit and clipping $30 from a grocery bill, gives a $70 raise for the month ($40 + $30 =$70)

Based on a savings of $70.00 you are prepared to rid yourself of debt. What you do is take a portion of that savings and apply it to a bill that can be paid off, such as a credit card.

For example:

If you have a credit card with a balance of $450.00 and your payment is $15.00 per month. It would take over 2 years to pay it off. So, what you do is take $35.00 of the $70.00 you saved, add the $35.00 to the $15.00 credit card payment, making the payment $50.00 a month. (this will allow the $35.00 to go straight to the principal balance of the credit card, thus paying the card off in one year. The other $35 from your ($70), can be applied to a bill or your savings, either move positions you for greatness.

These two techniques described are considered ways to power down your debt. Mastering the two will help you control your finances. Along with maintaining your savings and applying them to investments such as 401k and mutual funds (to be discussed further in Chapter 3).

By implementing any of the guidelines discovered in this section, you will notice a difference in your account and you will appreciate the new relationship with your finances in a few short months. Correcting your current financial situation will not happen overnight. When mastering financial control, patience is a necessity, so consider patience as virtue and while your goals are unfolding towards maturity, you will be over-joyed with the benefits from you keeping your financial records organized. Organization is the pavement you walk on in this journey.

TREASURE YOUR TREASURE

Don't spend the savings right away. Apply it to your plan to give life to your goals.

During my high school days, I was part of a state championship team and there was a time when our team was down in points by 2 possessions with only minutes left in the game. I remember our team having possession of the ball and rushing down the field for a huge score and we all celebrated. However, we were still down in points. The coach called time out, huddled us up and said "it's not time to celebrate, I'm glad you guys scored and that's good, but we don't have control of the score board yet, and for us to be great and take this victory home, we have to get control of the board."

I told this special little story to say this, "when you succeed in clipping $30 worth of saving from your grocery bill, DO NOT celebrate by going out to dinner with the savings (the old way of thinking would say, I have a little extra money. YOU DON'T!). The $30 is now your savings, it's an opportunity for you to power down your debt and take control of your finances. Don't spend (celebrate) your savings. Treasure your treasure (save your savings) and use part of your savings to get financial control. Note: using your savings to rid yourself of debt, is not spending your savings, it's getting financial control. Celebrating with your savings (doing what you want to do first, instead of doing what you need to do first), that's called spending.

My Money Plan

Creating a budget for your income is an important decision for your financial future. A budget is a spending plan that gives you foresight on where your money will be spent, before the money

lived and now it's time to pay for it. YOU CANNOT BUILD NET WORTH IF YOU DON'T GET RID OF THIS BAD DEBT NOW!

5. Next, determine your savings. In a good budget, this may be the most important, and first step. This concept is known as "Pay Yourself First"! The concept is simple – How much of my earnings can I keep? It can feel like everyone, everywhere is out to get your money. You have to decide who, and for what services, you are willing to give it up (your money). YOU WILL NEED MONEY IN THE FUTURE, SO PREPARE NOW! Saving for the future falls into several categories including:

   a. Emergency funds – This is your "what if" account. As the name suggests, these are not planned expenses, but for the unseen and unknown. What if you are unable to work for a period of time? What is something breaks down? Having an emergency fund keeps you from making your worst decisions like taking high interest loans and/or cashing in money making assets. We generally recommend between 3 to 6 months of expenses or income.
   b. Short term savings (1-3 years) – These funds are for coming expenses outside of normal budget. Items like vacation money, tires for your car, new furniture, Christmas/birthday presents, etc.
   c. Medium-term savings (3-10 years) – These accounts include: Saving for a down payment for a house, college funds, purchase a car, or other long term purchases.
   d. Lastly is long term savings (10 + years) – These accounts include retirement, college funding, inheritance planning etc.

6. Finally, don't get depressed! The bible says, "press toward the mark of the high call which is in Christ Jesus." He expects us to be good stewards over our finances, He wants us debt free. So, we have to press our way toward what's right, if we don't press we may get depressed.

comes. This plan gives you more control because it helps you determine if your income and expenses are balanced correctly. If they are not, you have the opportunity to make some adjustments and prioritize your expenses.

A budget gives you control over balancing your expenses with your income. Note: this should not be an equal balance, in fact your income should out-weigh your expenses. If you are spending more than you make, you are in financial trouble. If you are spending more than you make, your finances are sick. But no worries, there is a cure...a budget. Try one it's medicine for your finances. A budgeting plan may require you to change the way you think about money.

The challenge is how much can you save? Not how much do you make?

Building Your Budget

These are the main components of a budget:

1. Expected income – Is my income consistent? What can I count on weekly, monthly, annually? Be conservative. Don't expect that you can get overtime or extra bonuses every time you want them. What has your history taught you? Explore opportunities to make more income for future budgets, but DO NOT count on them until you have achieved them.

2. Determine and prioritize your fixed expenses. Things like housing, transportation, food, clothing, insurance, taxes, etc. Recognize the monthly that bills are due......monthly, quarterly, annually, etc.

3. Determine expected variable expenses such as utilities, gas, entertainment, healthcare, etc.

4. Determine debt payments (loans, credit cards, etc). These debt payments are paying for the life you have already

Understand that you may not immediately be able to do all the things listed above that you would like to. Most of us can't! These are the tough choices... What do I prioritize most? How do I balance needs for today with needs for the future. No one can answer these questions for you. You must choose, hmm, Do I value cable TV or eating out? Do I enjoy eating out or saving for a down payment for a house? Will I spend more on housing or more on transportation? THE CHOICE IS YOURS!

Once you create your budget, you'll see what's coming and what's going. Many people create plans for a month out, I encourage you to progress towards budgeting 3 to 6 months down the road. This route can help you pin-point spending habits. With your budgeting plan you can make spending adjustments and possibly provide an opportunity to plan ahead for big purchases or life changing events.

If you think you can't budget because your money isn't steady for whatever reason, try one of these techniques for financial control.

1. Budget Using Your Average Income. If this amount is not enough to meet all your expenses, you must consider how you can increase your income on a regular basis or decrease your expenses to make your budget balance, for instance: part time job, sell some of your stuff, internet business, etc.

2. Use Two Budgets: One for Good Times & Another for Leaner Times. You will have to be disciplined and detail oriented. It will be hard to manage your money this way. Be sure not to develop spending habits or supplement your income with credit spending because this behavior creates an expensive downward cycle towards bad debt and financial bondage and it is hard to break free of these monsters.

3. Envelope budget: this technique to me is considered old school. My parents used this system to manage the household dollars when I was a youngster. The budgeting techniques we discuss deal mainly with pen/paper and computer tracking methods. But, for some people, in the on start of their new financial discipline, this method may prove helpful. Ok, so after you have determined your expense

categories and spending limits for each, then get an envelope for each category and label it accordingly.

Example:

GAS

DEPOSIT   **SPENT**

_____ date ____   _____ date ____

_____ date ____   _____ date ____

_____ date ____   _____ date ____

The envelope system says, withdraw the cash from your checking account (according to the category spending limit) and put the money into each envelope category. For example: if your March spending budget for gas is ($100), then at the beginning of the month, if your budget allows, you can deposit $100 cash into the "gas" envelope or split it and take it from into 2 paychecks at ($50) each, or 4 paychecks at ($25)each, depending on your pay cycle. Be sure to stick with the budget limits you set for each category. Remember, you are practicing discipline and you want financial control. Do Not rob the Gas envelope to fund the entertainment envelope. In that first month, stick to your plan. The second month, you may notice a need to make some adjustments in some categories for the next month and that's ok. Adjustments may be necessary from month to month to achieve financial control.

This may prove to be a good accountability system for you and can work well with variable expenses. I recommend that you continue to pay your fixed expenses such as Mortgage/rent, car, insurance, cable, etc. thru your online bill pay or check or money order. Make sure you are keeping track of all your monetary transactions and recording them in their proper places.

I Believe

If you don't find the comfort of living within your means to be sufficient, then change your means first. You don't have to get there on Day One. But by establishing your goals and working in that direction, steadily and positively, you'll achieve a state of living within your means and ultimately be debt free with financial control. Now, let's get that money plan together.

Here are some budgeting Categories with the cost of living broken down into percentages of your income. Use these percentages as guidelines when creating your budget until you get control of your finances.

For instance: if clothing is part of your budget, 5-7% of your monthly net income may be spent on clothing. You may choose to budget below 5% or above 7% depending on what is most beneficial to you in your plan.

- **Clothing: 5 – 7%**
  cleaning-laundry/ new wardrobe

- **Food: 15 – 20%**
  groceries / restaurants

- **Debt Payments: 5 – 15%**
  debt is a form of bondage and many households find that their debt payments are closer to 25% of their net income. Which puts a humungous strain on the budget. Power down that debt and free yourself from this bondage.

- **Housing: 35%**
  insurance / mortgage / rent / taxes

- **Medical: 5-7%**
  co-pays / health care premiums/ medicines

- **Personal & Discretionary: 5 – 10%**
  entertainment / gaming / hobbies / recreation / salon (barber)

- **Savings & Investing: 5 – 15%**
  Having a surplus (savings) is a necessity for financial control. Once a savings is established you can then plan on investing. Your savings is important for emergencies or large repairs. Investing will set you up for a fabulous future. Plan to save money then you'll have a little extra available when you need it.

- **Transportation: 15 – 20%**
  bus / fuel / insurance / maintenance / parking/ uber

- **Utilities: 5%-10%**
  cable/ cell phone / gas & electric / internet

Here are some concepts and tips to maximize the effectiveness of managing your money.

1. Save early to save more – There are concepts called "Time value of Money" and the "Rule of 72". They show you how to earn more money simply because you saved first and spent later. The longer you have money invested, the more time it has to double and double and double.... You get the idea. For example, consider this: An investment of $1,000 at age 20 will grow to $32,000 by age 60 without ever adding to it (based on a 9% interest rate). What if a 20 year-old kept saving $1,000 every year from that point on.... The results could be amazing.

2. Maintain a good credit rating – Pay your bills on time, minimize the number of credit lines you have open. Not all loans are created equal. If you are in debt, get rid of the highest interest rates as soon as possible. High interest rates are slowing and destroying your ability to get ahead. They are designed to keep you in debt. The better your credit rating, the better your opportunity for lower interest ratings.

3. Interest Rate matters – Whether you are investing or borrowing, interest rates matter. Look for investments that match your timeline (time until you need the money) and your risk tolerance. If you have to borrow money, look for the lowest rates possible.

4. Learn about the various types of savings and investment accounts. Some of the biggest issues people face is by not knowing the best types of accounts for the specific

purpose for the money. For example, retirement accounts are generally for retirement and not for short-term expense. That's why you must have short-term savings. There is no "One Size Fits All" accounts.

5. If "free money" is being offered by your employer through matching contributions, don't ignore it.

6. Don't be limited by what your employer does or doesn't provide. If retirement is not offered, you can start your own. If insurance isn't provided, you can get you own. No excuses. The responsibility is on you.

7. Get the appropriate insurance to assist with the "What If's" in life. This should include, Car, House, life, disability, health insurance.

8. Make sure you have a Will to provide instructions for your wishes to be carried out concerning your possessions and the care of your minor children.

There are several budgeting apps available on the web and the app store, find one that suits you and simplifies your financial control journey. I've included a couple of manual budgeting work sheets to help you plow your way to financial control and a debt free life.

Weekly/Bi-Weekly Plan (The Budget)

There will be some months with an extra pay period. You can use this income to fund your savings or use it to power down one of your bills and rid yourself of debt.	Week Income 1			Week Income 2			Week Income 3			Week Income 4		
	$			$			$			$		
	$			$			$			$		
	$			$			$			$		
	$			$			$			$		
	Total			Total			Total			Total		

Clothing	Budget	Spent	$Left-over (+/-)	Budget	Spent	$Left-over (+/-)	Budget	Spent	$Left-over (+/-)	Budget	Spent	$Left-over (+/-)
Cleaning/laundry												
New wardrobe												
Total $	$	$		$	$	$	$	$	$	$	$	$

Debt Payments	Budget	Spent	$Left-over (+/-)	Budget	Spent	$Left-over (+/-)	Budget	Spent	$Left-over (+/-)	Budget	Spent	$Left-over (+/-)
Car Payment												
Car Payment												
Credit Card												
Other												
Other												
Total $	$	$		$	$	$	$	$	$	$	$	$

Food	Budget	Spent	$Left-over (+/-)	Budget	Spent	$Left-over (+/-)	Budget	Spent	$Left-over (+/-)	Budget	Spent	$Left-over (+/-)
Groceries												
Restaurants												
Total $	$	$		$	$	$	$	$	$	$	$	$

Giving	Budget	Spent	$Left-over (+/-)	Budget	Spent	$Left-over (+/-)	Budget	Spent	$Left-over (+/-)			
Charity												
Offering												
Tithes												
Total $	$	$										

Housing	Budget	Spent										
Mortgage/Taxes												

Monthly Plan (The Budget)

	First Income	Second Income	Other
Items here should include all pay stubs from a given month and all other routine income from the same month	_____	_____	_____
	_____	_____	_____
	_____	_____	_____
	_____	_____	_____
	_____	_____	_____
	_____	_____	_____
Totals	$_____	$_____	$_____

Monthly Totals 1st Inc. + 2nd Inc. + Other = $_____

FOOD the plan (15-20%) $_____

	Budget		Spent
Groceries	_____		_____
Restaurants	_____		_____
	(15-20%) $		Actual $

GIVING the plan (10-15%) $_____

SECTION 3

"Planning and Investing"

In this section we will be discussing some avenues available that will assist in securing your future through investing and planning. We will address the following items:

ESTATE PLANNING

In times passed, the notion of estate planning was thought to be a necessity only to the big ballers. Since then, we've come to realize, in order to be big, we cannot think small. Today the average income earner is exposed to a wealth of information and education about being savvy financial budgeteers and investors, even when we are starting with a little. So, because of all of your hard work and sticking to your budget and achieving your financial goals, we urge you to at a minimum, understand the basics of estate planning. This is a tool that will assist you in solidifying your future financial goals and ensure the integrity of your family's financial future is secure.

To achieve the greatest benefit from estate planning, you may have to rethink how you prioritize the milestones that may occur in your lifetime. For instance, there are people who spend more time planning birthday parties, anniversaries or even their vacations, than planning their estates. This may occur because these events bring current gratification. However, estate planning is important and requires much time and effort to achieve the goals set for you and your loved-ones (if we change the way we think about our finances we can change our future). Without a comprehensive estate plan, a significant part of the work you've done throughout your life, including acquiring your prize possessions and your investments, can be lost or given to unintended beneficiaries.

The purpose of estate planning is to prepare to transfer your assets to others upon your death. Estate planning gives you control as to where each of your assets go upon your death. This involves deciding who the beneficiaries will be, what each will get, and how to perform those transfers with the minimum tax burden, while making sure that the estate has enough liquidity to meet its obligations (expenses and/or liabilities).

Some components of an estate plan include last will and testament, living will, healthcare proxy, power of attorney, life insurance, and naming an executor/trustee.

Next is a questionnaire of vital information that you or a lawyer will need when preparing documents for estate planning.

Net Worth

It all starts with Net Worth

Simply stated, net worth is everything we have minus everything we owe. Your estate includes all the assets you own-such as investments, real estate and other property, cash, retirement accounts, life insurance policies, personal possessions, interest in a business, and anything else of value. If you have any debt, it should be subtracted from your assets to determine your overall net worth. Most people don't know the importance of this topic nor have they calculated their number. We all have a limited number of working years to earn an income to build our net worth. That net worth is what can eventually provide an income for us in the later years of life. Remember this theme – "Retirement is not an age, but a number." The sooner I build my net worth, the sooner I will be able to convert my net worth into income, which is the ultimate goal.

Calculate your lifetime earnings:

Part 1 in building Net Worth

How many working years will you have available? This question varies depending on a number of factors including:

1. The type of work I do. Are there longevity issues based on the physical nature of the profession (athletics, carpet layers, drywall, military, etc.)

2. Maintaining your health. The Council for Disability Awareness predicts 1 in 4 of current 20 years olds will become disabled prior to retirement.

Multiply your average expected earnings by the number of years you plan on working. This is your lifetime earning opportunity to build your net worth.

Example:

average expected earnings x # of years worked= lifetime earnings   .

$50,000   x   25 years   = $1,250,000 lifetime gross

Determine how you will spend your money:

Part 2 in building Net Worth

In speaking with consumers over the last 27 years, this is the point most neglected. Too many people could not tell you where their money goes. In fact, people often spend money in the areas of their lives that are not the highest priorities. This is where budgets come in. For most people, the idea of a budget has such a negative connotation that they avoid it at all cost. The truth is that a budget does not limit or keep you from spending money, but it insures that you use money for the most important priorities of your life.

Your ability to make informed choices before the temptations come will help you stay on track. People always believe that if they could make more money, then they could afford to have everything they want. Unfortunately, that simply is not the case. The want and desire for more is never satisfied. *Wisdom: (if you don't want anything you will have more money).*

We've proven as a society that we can spend large sums of money – no matter how much we earn!

Real estate is an important component in building net worth. Keep in mind that the seemingly simple concept of 'ownership' isn't always so simple. Sometimes an asset is owned by more than one person. For example, 'joint tenancy with right of survivorship' means that if one owner dies, the other becomes the full owner. 'Tenancy by the entirety' which only exists in some states, covers property owned jointly by spouses. And some states recognize 'community property' between spouses as distinct from separate property. Laws vary from one state to another, and the laws can be confusing, so be sure to know which laws apply to you if you own any shared property.

NET WORTH

<u>**ASSETS**</u>

CASH

Checking Accounts	$_____	**LIFE INSURANCE/ANNUITIES**	
Savings	$_____	Cash Value of Life Insurance	$_____
CD's	$_____	Surrender Value of Annuities	$_____
Savings Bonds	$_____		
Other	$_____	**CURRENT MARKET VALUE OF HOME(S)**	
		Primary Residence	$_____
RETIREMENT		Rental/Vacation Properties	$_____
401K's	$_____		
IRA's	$_____	**PROPERTY**	
Keogh Accounts	$_____	Antiques	$_____
Pensions	$_____	Boats	$_____
		Cars	$_____

OTHER INVESTMENTS/BROKERAGE ACCOUNTS

Stocks $_____

Bonds

As always, the information we provide is not an exhaustive study of the regulations and laws of your local municipality or state. Please consult a licensed CPA and an attorney concerning your specific business and situation.

Wills and Important Documents

There are three wills and other documents I want to discuss here: last will and testament, living will, codicil, power of attorney, and living trust. I believe each of these instruments are beneficial and essential to every estate plan. I recommend at a minimum that you include a last will and testament, a living will, and a power of attorney. These legal documents ensure that your wishes, your wealth, and your life legacy are all preserved and handled as you have planned.

Why have a will?

To clarify your wishes to your loved ones. Such as, appointing a guardian for your children or choosing a person to settle your affairs and deciding who will inherit your assets and property.

Having a will is extremely important. It is a written or typed document that must be signed and witnessed. This document will provide you with an opportunity to control how your assets and property will be distributed at the time of your death. If you do not have a will when you die, your assets and property will generally pass according to the state's laws of intestacy *(which means, if you don't have a will your state will make one for you. The purpose of the intestate statue is to distribute the decedent's wealth in a manner that closely represents how the general population would have designed their estate plan, had they had a will.)* All fifty states have intestacy laws. Each state's law may vary, and the statues that may apply to you are usually determined based on where you resided and/or where your property/asset is located.

In addition to giving you control over how you pass along your wealth, a will can generally be used to nominate a guardian for minor children, name a custodian, or guardian to hold or manage the assets of their minor children; also, name a personal representative for the estate and establish a trust upon your death such as a Bypass Trust or Special Needs Trust. A will is revocable (and you have that right) and you have the authority to amend your will at any time during your lifetime.

The Will and Probate

What is probate? It's when the courts make sure your debts are paid and your assets are distributed according to your will. If you don't have a valid will, your assets will be distributed according to state laws. This can be a lengthy process, usually nine months to two years. Assets can be frozen, and any movement of the assets has to have court approval. It can be a huge headache, not to mention costly, I'm talking legal fees, executor fees and other cost that will be paid out of the estate. Without a will, the estate, pretty much is at the mercy of the courts

KnowThis
Joint ownership doesn't always avoid probate. Be sure to discuss your state laws with a reputable attorney

NOTE: A will cannot be used to avoid probate or to distribute non-probate assets - such as life insurance policies and IRA accounts. In addition, a will cannot be used to disinherit a surviving spouse if he or she is entitled to a share of the estate based on your state's intestacy laws. Keep in mind that the seemingly simple concept of 'ownership' isn't always so simple. Sometimes an asset is owned by more than one person. For example, 'joint tenancy with right of survivorship' means that if one owner dies, the other becomes the full owner. 'Tenancy by the entirety', which only exists in some states, covers property owned jointly by spouses. Some states recognize 'community property' between spouses as distinct from separate property. Laws vary from one state to another, and the laws can be confusing, so be sure to know which laws apply to you if you own any shared property.

As always, the information provided is not an exhaustive study of the regulations and laws of your local municipality or state. Please consult a licensed CPA and an attorney concerning your specific business and situation.

I Believe
Regardless of how much you own, you need a will. If you want to control the distribution of your estate according to your wishes you must have a will; if you have minor children, it is absolutely a necessity to have a will so you can name a guardian for your child.

One more tip: *Whether you have a lot of assets or not much, whether you have minor children or not, do your loves ones a favor... prepare your end of life documents and make your wishes known!*

KnowThis
Most states require that you have two witnesses attest and sign your Will. Every state has its own requirements for the legality of your Will, so be sure to do your due diligence to know the requirements of your state. Check-out this list of states with the location of the state laws and execution requirements, locate your state and you can research the information through the internet. Example: for state laws, in the search window, type in [Alabama title 43 chapter 8]. Similarly, with execution Requirements, in the search window, type in [Alabama 43-8-131].

State	State Laws	Execution Requirements
Alabama	Title 43, Chapter 8	§ 43-8-131 Two Witnesses
Alaska	Title 13, Chapter 12	AS 13.12.502 Two Witnesses
Arizona	Title 14	§ 14-2502 Two Witnesses
Arkansas	Title 28	§ 28-25-102 Two Witnesses
California	Sections 6100 to 6139	6110 Two Witnesses
Colorado	CRS Title 15	§ 15-11-502 Two Witnesses or Notary Public
Connecticut	Chapter 802a	Section 45a-251 Two Witnesses
Delaware	Title 12	DE Title 12, Chapter 2 § 201 & 202 Two Witnesses
Florida	Chapter 732	FL Section 732.502 Two Witnesses
Georgia	Title 53	GA Section 53-4-20 Two Witnesses
Hawaii	Chapter 560	HI Section 560:2-502 Two Witnesses
Idaho	Title 15	ID Section 15-2-502 Two Witnesses
Illinois	755 ILCS 5	Section 755 ILCS 5/4-3 Two Witnesses
Indiana	Title 29	IC 29-1-5-3 Two Witnesses
Iowa	Chapter 633	Section 633.279 Two Witnesses

State	State Laws	Execution Requirements
Kansas	Chapter 59	Section 59-606 Two Witnesses
Kentucky	Chapter 394	Section 394.040 Two Witnesses
Louisiana	CC 1570	Art. 1577 Two Witnesses and a Notary Public
Maine	Title 18-A, Article 2	Section 2-502 Two Witnesses
Maryland	Title 4	Section 4-102 Two Witnesses
Massachusetts	Chapter 190B	Section 2-502 Two Witnesses
Michigan	Act 386 of 1998	Section 700-2502 Two Witnesses
Minnesota	Chapter 524	Section 524.2-502 Two Witnesses
Mississippi	Title 91, Chapter 5	Section 91-5-1 Two Witnesses
Missouri	Title XVI	Section 474.320 Two Witnesses
Montana	Title 72	Section 72-2-522 Two Witnesses
Nebraska	Chapter 30	Section 30-2327 Two Witnesses
Nevada	Title 12	NRS 133.040 Two Witnesses
New Hampshire	Chapter 551	Section 3B:3-2 Two Witnesses
New Jersey	Title 3B	Section 3B:3-2 Two Witnesses

State	State Laws	Execution Requirements
New Mexico	Chapter 45	Section 45-2-502 Two Witnesses
New York	Estates, Powers, and Trusts	Section 3-1.1 Two Witnesses
North Carolina	Chapter 31	G.S. 31-3.3 Two Witnesses
North Dakota	Chapter 30.1-08	30.1-08-02. (2-502) Two Witnesses
Ohio	Chapter 2107	ORC 2107.03 Two Witnesses
Oklahoma	Title 84	84 OK Stat § 84-55 Two Witnesses
Oregon	Chapter 112	ORS 112.235 Two Witnesses
Pennsylvania	Title 20	Title 20 § 2502 Two Witnesses
Rhode Island	Title 33	Section 33-5-5 Two Witnesses
South Carolina	Title 62	Section 62-2-502 Two Witnesses
South Dakota	Chapter 29A-1	Section 29A-2-502 Two Witnesses
Tennessee	Title 32	Section 32-1-104 Two Witnesses
Texas	Probate Code	Sec. 251.051 Two Witnesses
Utah	Title 75	75-2-502 Two Witnesses
Vermont	Title 14	14 V.S.A. § 5 Two Witnesses

Codicil

How to Amend a Will? You could redo the entire will (which may be the absolute best way to amend your will), but you could also insert an amendment known as a **"codicil"**, which is not un-common and most cost effective. A codicil allows you to change certain portion of the will without rewriting the entire document. Like the will the codicil has to be signed and dated by the testator according to state laws and it must have two (2) witness with no interest in the outcome of the will.

KnowThis

- *Anything that's in joint name or payable to a named beneficiary, such as life insurance policies or 401(k) balances, is outside the scope of a will*
- *So, I say, you should assign beneficiaries for as many accounts as possible. (you can do this with the institution that holds your account)*
- *You can also create transfer-on-death or payable-on-death designations for checking, savings, and money market accounts, as well as certificates of deposit and U.S. bonds. Establishing these designations allows your beneficiary to collect funds without having to go through probate court. (again, check with the institution)*
- *The state you have listed as your primary residence will govern your Will.*

The next few pages list a sample Last Will and Testament.

LAST WILL AND TESTAMENT OF

_____(name)

I, _____, an
adult whose address is at

_____

_____, being of sound mind, declare this to be my Last Will
and Testament. I revoke all wills and codicils previously made by
me.

I am married, my spouses name is

_____

I have _____ child(ren)

Name   Address   Date of Birth

_____   _____   _____

_____   _____   _____

_____   _____   _____

_____   _____   _____

_____   _____   _____

_____   _____   _____

_____   _____   _____

ARTICLE I

I appoint _____ ,whose address
is_____ _____as
my Personal Representative/Executor to serve without bond and
administer this will. If unable to serve, I appoint
_____, whose address is
_____, as my
Alternate Representative/Executor, also to serve without bond and
administer this will. To the named representative I grant any and all of
my powers necessary to perform any acts, in his/her sole discretion and
ask that the appointed person be permitted to serve without Court
supervision.

ARTICLE II

I direct my Personal Representative to pay out of my residuary estate all
of the expenses of my last illness, administration expenses, all legally
enforceable creditor claims, all Federal estate taxes, state inheritance
taxes, and all other governmental charges imposed by reason of my
death without seeking reimbursement from or charging any person for
any part of the taxes and charges paid, and if necessary, reasonable
funeral expenses, including the cost of any suitable marker for my
grave, without the necessity of an order of court approving said
expenses.

ARTICLE III

I devise, bequeath, and give my

_____,

_____, to

_____.

I devise, bequeath, and give my

_____ ,

_____ , to

_____ .

I devise, bequeath, and give my

_____ ,

_____ , to

_____ .

ARTICLE IV

I devise, bequeath, and give all the rest and remainder of my residuary estate as follows:

1. _____ %
   to_____

2. _____ %
   to_____

3. _____ %
   to_____

ARTICLE V

Should any beneficiary not survive me by _____ days, their share shall be

_____

_____

_____

Here are more samples of important forms, you can find complete forms in the workbook, sold separately.

LAST WILL AND TESTAMENT OF

_____(name)

I, _____, an adult whose address is at
_____. being of
sound mind, declare this to be my Last Will and Testament. I revoke all wills and codicils previously made by me.

I am married, my spouses name is _____

I have _____ child(ren)

Name	Address	Date of Birth
_____	_____	
_____	_____	
_____		
_____		
_____		

SELF-PROVING AFFIDAVIT

I publish and sign this last will and testament, consisting of _____typewritten pages, on
_____, 20_____, and I declare that I do so freely, for the purposes expressed. I am under no constraint or undo influence, and I am of sound mind and of legal age.

_____   _____
Signature of Testator   Printed Name of Testator

We the undersigned and witnesses, being first sworn on oath and under penalty of perjury, state that:

1. That the Testator executed this instrument as his Will:
2. That in the presence of witnesses, the Testator signed or acknowledge his signature already made, or directed another to sign for him in his presence:
3. That the Testator executed the Will as his free and voluntary act for the purposes expressed in it:
4. That each of the witnesses, in the presence of the Testator and of each other, signed the Will as a witness:

CODICIL TO LAST WILL AND TETSTAMENT OF

_____(name)

I _____, residing at _____.

_____, being of sound mind, declare

this Codicil to my Last Will and Testament dated_____, 20_____,

Is effective as of today, _____, 20_____.

Amendment l

Article _____ of my Will shall be modified to read:

_____

_____

_____

Amendment ll

Article _____ of my Will shall _____:

_____

_____

_____

Amendment lll

Article _____ of my Will shall

Living Will (Advance Healthcare Directive)

A Living Will is another important activity that gives you power to make decisions about your future healthcare. It's certainly not the same type of Will whereby you leave heir-looms and real estate. It is actually a legal document where you can express your wishes concerning end of life medical treatments and procedures you want or don't want. A living will (advance healthcare directive) is used in the event your health becomes critical and you are unable to make those decisions on your own. I know this is not the most exciting thing to talk about, but discussing this issue affords you the opportunity to make future healthcare decisions now at a time when your life is not threatened and you're thinking clearly. When you create a living will it specifies such things as the use of life-sustaining procedures and artificially provided nutrition. This is where you express your wishes about measures taken to preserve or not to preserve your life. This is where you can determine what happens to you (God Forbid) if you are needing a ventilator, if your heart stops, if you can't eat or any other incapacitating illness which may not allow you to verbalize your wishes effectively. In the absence of a living will your loved ones would have to make difficult decisions about your care and possibly life-saving interventions, without your input. Having a living will can prevent you from placing that great burden on your loved ones. Again, a living will gives you control over the type of treatment you want and the type of procedures you would like to have as end of life care.

Understand a living will explains your wishes and informs health care providers of what measures they should use to prolong your life or to cease life-sustaining measures. A living will covers one stage of your life, and that's when you're near death. So, you can also incorporate a legal document known as an advance medical directive and with this you can designate someone else to make health care decisions on your behalf if you are unable to do so yourself.

Note: this can also be accomplished using a durable power of attorney for healthcare.

If you don't have any of these documents set up, the state laws will make these important decisions for you if you ever can't do it on your own.

KnowThis

You have rights under the HIPAA law concerning your healthcare information. "The Privacy Rule, a Federal law, gives you rights over your health information and sets rules and limits on who can look at and receive your health information. The Privacy Rule applies to all forms of individuals' protected health information, whether electronic, written, or oral. The Security Rule is a Federal law that requires security for health information in electronic form."

Your rights:

- *You can see or get a copy of your records*
- *You can have corrections made to your records*
- *You can give permission or deny your information being shared for certain purposes*
- *Your medical records are protected, your conversations with yours doctors, billing info, etc.*
- *Your Doctors, nurses, Health insurance companies, HMO's, Pharmacies, nursing homes, etc., must follow this law*

If you believe your rights are being violated or denied you can file a complaint with your health insurer, your provider or the U.S. government (visit: www.hhs.gov/hipaa/for-individuals/guidance-materials-for-consumers/index.html)

I Believe

whether you have a lot of assets or not much, whether you have minor children or not, you should do your loved ones a favor... prepare your end of life documents and make your wishes known!

LIVING WILL (HEALTHCARE DIRECTIVE)

If the time comes when I can no longer take part in decisions for my own healthcare, let this declaration stand as my spoken word and my wishes concerning my future healthcare treatment.

Declaration made the _____ day of _____ , 20 _____ .

(Declarant's name)_____ (DOB) _____

(address)_____(city, state & zip)_____

Part A

I _____ (Declarant), being of a sound mind, willfully and voluntarily make known my desire to die peacefully and not artificially prolong the process.

_____(initial) I hereby declare that if at anytime it is determined I have an incurable disease, illness or injury that is certified to be a terminal condition by 2 physicians who has examined me, one being my attending physician, and the 2 physicians have determined that my death will occur whether or not life sustaining procedures are used and the use of life-sustaining procedures would serve only to artificially prolong the dying process, then, I direct that such procedures be withheld or withdrawn, and that I be permitted to die naturally with only the administration of medication or medical procedure deemed necessary to provide me with comfort care.

_____(initial) I do not want to be on a breathing machine

_____(initial) I do not want a feeding tube

_____(initial) If I die do not resuscitate me (DNR)

Part B

I understand that when I die, I can donate my organs. I wish to donate the organs I have listed below._____(initials)

_____

_____

Part C

DURABLE POWER OF ATTORNEY FOR HEALTH CARE
(DESIGNATION OF HEALTH CARE SURROGATE)

In the event that I _____, Age_____ have been determined by my phsycian(s) to be incompetent/incapacitated (lack the ability) to provide informed consent for medical treatment and surgical procedures including but not limited to the withholding, withdrawal, or continuation of life prolonging procedures, I wish to designate as my decision maker (surrogate) to make health care decisions for me:

Name:_____/_____Phone#(w)_____
                                                relationship   (c)_____

Address:_____

If my surrogate is unwilling or unable to perform his/her duties. I wish to designate as my alternate decision maker:

Name:_____/_____Phone#(w)_____
                                                relationship   (c)_____

Address:_____

I fully understand that this designation will permit my decision maker to make all healthcare decisions on my behalf until I regain the ability to make healthcare decisions for myself. The healthcare decisions made by my surrogate may include; the decisions to withhold, withdraw, or continue life prolonging procedures. My surrogate (decision-maker) may also authorize my admission to or transfer from a mental healthcare facility and also apply for public assistance on my behalf. This designation is to remain in place during any incompetency or incapacity I may experience.

Additional instructions (optional):

_____

_____

_____

_____

_____

LIVING TRUST

You may consider drafting a living trust if you have substantial assets, business interests involving partnerships and/or property in other states or complex personal circumstances, such as blended families or if you want to avoid probate court. A living trust is a tool that will provide you control over your assets during your lifetime and at your death. You can appoint a trustee to service your trust (but stay involved), or you can choose to serve as your own trustee (recommended) and at your death or incapacity, you set the trust to provide for a "successor trustee." (be sure to appoint someone you trust)

Unlike a will, a living trust can avoid probate at death and prevent the court from controlling your assets even if you become incapacitated. In layman's terms, a living trust is like a living person, it's a mini You. For example, when you set up a living trust, you transfer assets from *your* name to the name of *your* trust, which *you* control -- such as from "Me and You Jones, husband and wife" to "Me and You Jones", trustees under trust dated (month/day/year).

So legally, you no longer own the assets, your trust does. Therefore, there is nothing for the courts to control if you become incapacitated or die.

Note that assets have to be transferred into the trust before they can be serviced through the trust. You have the option of transferring titles on bank accounts, CDs, insurance, investments, real estate, stocks, and other assets with titles. Also feel free to include art, clothes, furniture, jewelry, and other assets that don't have titles.

The trust also has to be funded in order to handle the financial obligation that may be due, such final bills, real estate taxes, and federal estate taxes. (Your state may also have its own death or inheritance tax.) If you are married, your living trust can include a provision that will let you and your spouse use both of your exemptions, saving a substantial amount of money for your loved ones.
In the event of your death, the successor trustee will be responsible for paying all final expenses for the estate, such as, the final bills, debts, and taxes. The trustee will also make sure that the remaining assets will be dispersed according to your wishes.

Revocable trust: A revocable Living Trust allows you to transfer assets into the name of the trust, which allows you to avoid probate. However, you have the option of being the trustee, which puts you in direct control over the assets placed into the trust. This option gives you the flexibility to be the trustee or the beneficiary. You can remove assets, rewrite any of the terms of the trust or even change beneficiaries. While this position gives you flexibility, it's the same as ownership. With ownership in a living trust, your assets can avoid probate, but they may be subject to lawsuits and you will incur estate tax.

Irrevocable Trust: Unlike a revocable living trust, once assets have been transferred into a irrevocable trust, they cannot been changed or dissolved by the creator of the trust (the grantor). When you transfer assets into this irrevocable trust you (the grantor/ creator) no longer own the assets, they belong to the trust. At this juncture you will utilize an independent trustee to manage your trust. With an independent trustee you generally cannot change beneficiaries, reclaim assets, or change the terms of the trust.

Note: during the initial creation of the irrevocable trust you are in full control of the assets you are willing to put into the trust (and give up ownership), you are also in full control of the beneficiary selection (you can be a beneficiary of your trust), and you set the terms of the trust.

With this irrevocable trust, estate tax liability may be less (by transferring property into this type of trust (you have no ownership or control) it's out of your taxable estate, therefore reducing your tax liability, which allows you to transfer more accumulated wealth to your beneficiaries. You can also avoid probate, and you may be protected from creditors. Note: some are using their irrevocable trust to avoid Medicare nursing home spend-down, whereby a person needing nursing home services would have to spend all cash on hand and in some cases liquidate assets. When assets are in this trust, it may benefit the grantor in this situation. **(be sure to discuss this with your planner and investigate all regulations involving Medicare spend-down)**

Note: An Independent Trustee is one who does not benefit from the trust and does operate with oversight. The law requires all trustees to act independently and impartially, imposing stringent duties and liabilities. A trustee is required to always exercise their powers in the best interests of the beneficiaries. A trustee should always be prudent in managing the trust assets. Failure to perform this essential level of care will constitute a breach of trust, therefore the trustee will be liable to compensate the beneficiaries, and a trustee is not allowed to use the trust assets for personal gain, directly or indirectly. (You can also hire a trust protector, who monitors the independent trustee, who can hire and fire at will and set spending limits on how much the trustee is authorized to spend without a second signature. **(be sure to consult with your planner and a trust attorney for all regulations in your state)**

Power of Attorney

POA is a legal document, allowing you (the principal) to give someone (an agent) (whomever you choose) the authority to make decision on your behalf in specified matters or all financial and/or legal matters. Assigning someone as power of attorney (POA) is a big deal. It's a responsibility given to someone you trust to handle your business as you would. This person has a fiduciary duty. Which means that person (agent) is bound to act in your best interest not their own.

Power of attorney documents can be structured to give someone authority in many different areas personally, financially and legally. Below you'll find POA's you can consider to manage your affairs.

Durable Power of attorney: This POA provides greater flexibility. You spell out what powers you will transfer to the agent. With a durable power of attorney, the agent (whom you've give power to) will continue managing your affairs even if you become unable to manage your own affairs (incapacitated). For example, the durable power of attorney would enable the agent to pay your bills from your accounts, manage your property, manage your investments and manage and meet other obligations spelled out in the POA document, while you (the principal) are incapacitated. Having this type of POA can help avoid catastrophic results and prevent your family from pursuing a court order just to handle your business.

<u>General power of attorney:</u> a general power of attorney conveys a broad-base of powers, which are to be spelled out in the POA document. Unlike the durable power, the general POA terminates once the principal becomes incapacitated or dies.

<u>Limited power of attorney:</u> a limited power of attorney delegates one or more powers to the agent, such as handling a real estate transaction.

<u>Medical power of attorney:</u> a medical power of attorney allows you to give someone you trust (agent/surrogate), the authority to make medical decisions concerning your health care if you become incapacitated. Note: A living will is similar to a medical POA, the caveat is that the designated POA has the authority to change your wishes in the living will, since the power of attorney essentially authorizes the same power to the agent as if he or she is you.

<u>Springing power of attorney:</u> a springing power of attorney (similar to a durable POA) allows you to choose someone you trust (agent/ surrogate/attorney-in-fact) to manage your affairs if certain conditions occur. These conditions are spelled out in the POA, such being, incapacitated, comatose, or even military deployment. This POA will spring into effect if the condition set by the you (the principal) occurs.

I Believe
Having a Power of attorney will be a very beneficial and important tool in your estate plan. I believe you would rather not have your family petitioning the courts for the authority to handle your medical decisions or manage your estate. Going through the courts could be a long process (maybe to long medically) and it's possible the family may not receive favorable results. So, at a minimum be sure to create a power of attorney along with a living will and a last will and testament. Equip your estate and your family with the tools needed to honor and preserve your health and the wealth you have worked so hard to acquire and maintain.

GENERAL DURABLE POWER OF ATTORNEY

THE POWERS YOU GRANT BELOW ARE EFFECTIVE
ONLY IF YOU BECOME DISABLED OR INCOMPETENT

NOTICE: The powers granted by this document are broad and sweeping. They are explained in the uniform statutory form of power of attorney act. If you have any questions about powers, seek competent legal advice. This document does not authorize anyone to make medical and other health care decisions for you. You may consider a medical power of attorney if you later wish to do so. (page 68)

I _____

_____ (insert your name and address) appoint _____

_____ (insert name and address of person appointed)

my Agent (attorney-in-fact) to act for me in any lawful way with respect to the following

initialed subjects:

To grant all of the following powers, initial the line in front of (N) And ignore the lines in front of the other powers.

To grant one or more, But fewer than all of the following powers, initial the line in front of each power you are granting.

To withhold a power, Do Not initial the line in front of it. You may, but need not, cross out each power withheld.

Note: If you initial items L, M, or N a notarized signature will be required on behalf of the Principal.

Initial

_____ (A) **Banking another financial institution transaction.** To make, receive, sign, execute, acknowledge, deliver and possess checks, drafts, bills of exchange, let stock certificates, withdrawal receipts and deposit instruments relating to in, or certificates of deposit of banks, savings and association. To sue of any, if necessary

Get *"Living Your Best Life **Workbook** "* for all forms and lists

Next Steps

1. <u>Write the will:</u> a simple will should be easy. There is a template in the "living your best life workbook." You can also search online templates, computer software and internet apps that you can utilize to help you accomplish this journey. **Be sure to consult with a licensed insurance agent, CPA's and attorneys for all your questions and regulations for your state.**

2. <u>Living will:</u> write your living will. You can do it. If you're married discuss it with your spouse, let your thoughts be known about your health care and end of life wishes. Now, put it on paper.

3. <u>Establish a POA</u>: which ever one suits your needs (you can change or revoke your POA whenever you wish, it's your right.)

4. <u>Make sure your documents are legal:</u> wills must have state required language. Generally, what you need to execute a valid will is to be of sound mind and over the age of 18. You and a witness must sign and date the will (most state laws say that the witness should be disinterested, meaning they should not be a beneficiary and probably not a close relative, in a case like this the court could declare the will void). The witness should provide their full name and address in case they are needed for solidifying the will. POA's should be notarized.

5. <u>Make a copy:</u> (well, two copies) and keep them in a safe place (s) and give a copy to your agent and surrogate

6. <u>Do Not:</u> put the only copy in a safe deposit box! Your living will and your healthcare POA should be readily available. Let a couple of people know where your documents are stored.

7. <u>Make sure your documents stay updated:</u> you have control, remember, when things change in your life, be sure to revisit your wills and POA's.

Insurance Coverage

This is another opportunity whereby you solidify health and wealth plans for now and well into the future. This should also be included in your estate planning. Insurance provides a layer of protection to our assets, our income and to our dependents from financial loss. With this vehicle, we're able to transfer the risk of a substantial financial loss to an insurance company in return for payment of an affordable premium. Here are some types of insurances to consider:

- **Critical illness insurance:** provides a source of funds to help cover the indirect costs that arise when a serious illness strikes.

- **Disability insurance:** replaces income lost in the event of an accident or illness.

- **Health insurance:** helps to cover the cost of medical care (be sure it includes prescription cost)

- **Life insurance:** protects dependents from loss of income in the event of a breadwinner's death and it helps to pay cash needs that arise at death. There are many types of life insurance policies to choose from, below is a list of categories and types you can familiarize yourself with, so you can customize the right coverage for your family.

   1. **Term:** the simplest and most affordable of life insurance. The coverage is for an elected period of time and only offers protection at death and has no cash value build up. The amount elected at initiation is paid at death (death benefit).

   2. **Permanent:** Offers both a death benefit and has a cash value component (you can borrow money from the policy). It is also intended to provide coverage for the remainder of the insured's life as long as the premium is paid. Here are some types of permanent insurances:

      - **Whole life:** this is the simplest permanent life insurance, the premium is locked in for the life of the policy (makes budgeting consistent). This insurance offers a minimum guaranteed death benefit and it build cash value (at a minimum guaranteed rate of return) on a tax-deferred basis.

- **Universal life:** provides a death benefit and a cash value where some of your premiums can grow tax-deferred. It differs from Whole life in that the policy holder is allowed to move funds between the cash value component and the insurance component of the policy (you can increase the death amount during the life of the policy. Like the whole life you withdraw cash for other expenses.

- **Variable Universal life:** this also offers a death benefit and builds cash value. The Variable gives you the opportunity to try different investment options such as equities.

- **Index Universal life insurance:** this type of insurance gives a death benefit and provides a way for your funds to grow aggressively. Here part of your premium is invested in a fund that is driven by the index, generally the S&P 500, if the index does well so do your funds. Of course, the more you pay in premiums the faster you build your cash fund. The caveat is most insurances like this have high commissions and are often front-loaded so it could take years before seeing significant growth.

3. **Final Expense Life Insurance:** covers the cost of anything associated with your death, including cremation, funeral cost and medical bills. Coverage is usually in amounts from $5000 to $25,000. This type of life insurance generally carry high premiums for relatively low coverage amounts, but if your family's savings can't handle the burden of funeral cost this may be a vehicle to consider.

4. **No Exam Life Insurance:** also known as *"Simplified issue life insurance"* there is no medical exam for this insurance, but you do have to fill out a medical questionnaire. They want to know pretty much everything about you, illnesses, habits, etc. If they determine you are in poor health, they may require an exam or deny you. With this type of insurance comes high premiums as well.

5. **Group Life Insurance:** generally offered through an

72

employer, this is commonly term insurance (although it could be whole life. be sure). In many cases employers may offer it at no cost to you, take it, but don't stop there be sure you have adequate coverage to protect your family, income, and assets.

6. **Long-term care insurance:** helps to pay the costs of assisted living care or extended nursing home care.

7. **Property and casualty insurance:** it indemnifies (compensates) for losses to homes and cars, as well as provides liability protection.

KnowThis
I have listed basic overviews of some different types of insurance possibilities, again this is not an exhaustive description of these insurance categories. Please be sure to do an exhaustive inquiry of each insurance you may be interested in and consult with a licensed insurance agent and your financial advisor to discuss the pro's and con's of the insurance investment products.

I Believe
The type and amount of insurance you need is best determined by an analysis of your financial and your personal situation, as well as your financial goals and objectives. Be sure to have enough insurance to protect your dependents, your income and your assets.

FEATURES	BASIC TERM LIFE	BASIC WHOLE LIFE	UNIVERSAL LIFE	VARIABLE UNIVERSAL
Duration	1 - 30 years	Life	Life	Life
Guaranteed Death Benefit	Yes	Yes	Yes	Yes
Guaranteed Cash Value	N/A	Yes	Protected from risk, but can be depleted to pay premiums	No
How Cash Value Grows (or Shrinks)	N/A	Earns interest at a predetermined fixed rate	Variable rate determined by the insurer	Subaccounts - pool of investor funds offered by the insurer
Premiums	Can increase periodically or stay at a guaranteed level for the policy duration	Level	Varies, up to the customer (subject to federal tax laws)	Varies, up to the customer (subject to federal tax laws)
Notes	No risk of losing coverage, but no cash value when term ends	No risk compared to other permanent types, but you may find better investment options elsewhere	N/A	Risk of ending up with expensive insurance policy with little-to-no cash value

Taxes and Your Money

Understanding the importance and benefit of working with a tax professional or CPA with extensive tax experience, makes "cents"...

If you are like most people, taxes can be a source of stress and confusion. Working with a licensed tax professional can make the process easier and give you a more positive experience.

While you may have completed several of your own tax returns in your lifetime, a tax professional has completed thousands of returns and has dealt with a multitude of complicated situations. This experience can be invaluable to you if you are trying to optimize your tax situation and avoid paying too much in taxes. Everyone is different, so it is important to have an advisor that can help you navigate through your individual tax needs.

KnowThis
The Volunteer Income Tax Assistance (VITA) program offers free tax help to people who generally make $54,000 or less, persons with disabilities and limited English speaking taxpayers who need assistance in preparing their own tax returns. IRS-certified volunteers provide free basic income tax return preparation with electronic filing to qualified individuals.

What I want from my tax preparer & What to avoid.

A good tax preparer should be able to demonstrate expertise in the rules of taxation. They should be able to explain issues that affect your return in a clear way so that you can understand the impact of how things are reported. A preparer should have strong organizational skills and be able to provide you with source documents that agree to what is reported in the tax return. Be sure to check your accountant's credentials.

Avoid using an out of state CPA. State and local tax laws are different in every state and every county, city, municipality. A CPA will be more educated about the laws of their own state than they will of other states. Many CPAs who prepare taxes for another state may miss important deductions or credits due to their lack of experience in your state.

It is also important to avoid using a "Tax Preparation Firm" as opposed to a CPA firm. A CPA firm must be owned and operated by a CPA. CPAs require continued education to maintain their licenses and are often more knowledgeable than tax preparers. Avoid firms that are seasonal and not open all year round, use a reputable firm who will produce a copy of your return for you.

Avoid using a tax preparer who charges based on a percentage of your refund. Avoid using a tax preparer who promises a bigger refund than their competitors.

Important things to know when preparing your own taxes.

If you plan to prepare your own return, you should be sure you understand how to read your tax return and how to research tax issues. Often, self-prepared returns are done via store bought or online software. While these programs can help you to mechanically report your information, they do not interpret tax laws and are not guaranteed to produce an accurate return. When you sign your tax return, you are stating to the IRS that your return is complete and accurate. It is important to feel confident that you have prepared your return correctly.

Income tax bracket

Rate	For Unmarried Individuals, Taxable Income Over	For Married Individuals Filing Joint Returns, Taxable Income Over	For Heads of Households, Taxable Income Over
10%	$0	$0	$0
12%	$9,950	$19,900	$14,200
22%	$40,525	$81,050	$54,200
24%	$86,375	$172,750	$86,350
32%	$164,925	$329,850	$164,900
35%	$209,425	$418,850	$209,400
37%	$523,600	$628,300	$523,600

Can I take standard deduction? Who itemizes? If I don't, can I still take deductions?

All individuals are entitled to claim a standard deduction on their tax return. This deduction is used to offset some of your adjusted gross income when calculating your taxable income. There are several expenses (including medical expenses greater than 7 1/2% of AGI, state and local income taxes, real estate taxes, mortgage interest and charitable deductions) that are eligible for deduction. If they total more than the standard deduction then you may itemize. You should always calculate the total of your deductions eligible for itemization in order to take the maximum possible deduction. You are eligible to deduct the higher of the two.

Note: if either of you or your spouse or both were born before January 2, 1956 or if either of you or both are blind, then your standard deduction will increase.

Refer to IRS Publication 17

Filing Status	Deduction Amount
Single	$12,550
Married Filing Jointly	$25,000
Married filing separate	$12,500
Head of Household	$18,800
Qualifying Widow(er)	$25,100

What is Alternative Minimum Tax (AMT)?

The Alternative Minimum Tax is a mandatory alternative to the standard income tax. It gets triggered when taxpayers make more than the exemption and use many common itemized deductions. The tax is meant to keep certain high income taxpayers from paying less than their fair share of taxes due to having excessive eligible deductions compared to average taxpayers. This parallel tax income system requires high-income taxpayers to calculate their tax bill twice: once under the ordinary income tax system and again under the AMT.

Filing Status	Exemption Amount
Unmarried Individuals	$73,600
Married Filing Jointly	$114,600

The AMT uses an alternative definition of taxable income called Alternative Minimum Taxable Income (AMTI). To prevent low- and middle-income taxpayers from being subjected to the AMT, taxpayers are allowed to exempt a significant amount of their income from AMTI. However, this exemption phases out for high-income taxpayers. AMT exemptions phase out at 25 cents per dollar earned once taxpayer AMTI hits a certain threshold. In 2020, the exemption will start phasing out at $518,400 in AMTI for single filers and $1,036,800 for married taxpayers filing jointly.

The AMT is levied at two rates: 26 percent and 28 percent. In 2020, the 26 & 28 percent AMT rate applies to excess AMTI of $197,900 for all taxpayers ($98,950 for married couples filing separate returns).

Do I qualify for Earned Income Tax Credit (EITC)?

In order to qualify for the EITC, you must have earned income and adjusted gross income within certain limits and you must meet certain basic rules regarding your filing status. If you have qualifying children, the amount of your EITC will be higher.

Refer to IRS Publication 596

Filing Status	Single or Head of Household		Married Filing Jointly	
	Income at Max Credit	Maximum Credit	Income at Max Credit	Maximum Credit
No Children	$15,980.00	$543.00	$21,920.00	$543.00
One Child	$42,158.00	$3,618.00	$48,108.00	$3,618.00
Two Children	$47,915.00	$5,980.00	$53,865.00	$5,980.00
Three or More Children	$51,464.00	$6,728.00	$57,414.00	$6,728.00

What are some deductions or credits that might be available for 2020?

- **Student loans** - The maximum amount of student loan deduction is $2,500. Eligible student loan interest is reported to the taxpayer on Form 1099E.

- **Foreign earned income** - The foreign earned income exclusion for 2021 is $108,700. You must meet certain rules to be eligible to claim the exclusion.

- **IRA contributions** - The maximum IRA contributions for 2020 is $6,000. Depending on your individual tax situation, you may be eligible to contribute to a traditional IRA or a Roth IRA. (over 50 $7000)

- **Child/dependent care credit** - The maximum credit is worth up to $3,000/one child. For two children up to $6,000 of qualifying expenses. If you only have one child, the maximum is between 20-35% of $3,000 of qualifying expenses.

- **Adoption credit** - The maximum adoption credit is $14,440.

- **American Opportunity Tax Credit** - The American opportunity tax credit (AOTC) is a credit for qualified education expenses paid for an eligible student for the first four years of higher education. You can get a maximum annual credit of $2,500 per eligible student.

- **Lifetime learning credit** - The credit is worth 20% of eligible costs up to $10,000 (maximum $2,000).

- **Qualified Business Income (QBI) deduction** - The QBI is available for taxpayers that own their own business. Based on income and business type restrictions, you may be eligible to deduct 20% of your taxable business income.

- **Elective Contribution limits** - The maximum amount of 401k contributions and eligible participant can make in 2020 is $19,500. You can contribute an additional $6,500 per year if you are over age 50. Contributions are made on a pre-tax basis and reduce federal taxable wages on your W-2. Contributions are reported as code D in Box 12 of the W-2.

- **Flexible spending accounts** - The maximum FSA contribution for 2021 is $2,750.

KnowThis
Be sure to check for updated regulations each tax season. Don't assume your tax professional will always inform you of the changes in the tax laws. Always ask questions and seek information concerning your money and taxes.

General Advice about Taxes and Tax Preparation

The tax return that your CPA prepares is YOUR tax return, not your CPAs – If something is reported inaccurately, the IRS holds you accountable, not your CPA. Be sure to have your CPA educate you on your return so that you fully understand it and can attest to its accuracy. If there is something you do not understand, ask. Your CPA is the person signing the return and certifying their work, but you are the one who is liable for unreported or incorrect items.

Keep it simple, Make it easy – Throughout the year keep a clean record of your tax information. This means keeping an ongoing record of expenses, donations, education expenses, investment information, qualified accounts, additional income, miles driven, real estate taxes, mortgage interest, and all other tax items. Use an Excel spreadsheet to keep everything in one place and use Excel to produce totals. The less time your CPA has to take digging through items and calculating totals the less time it will take to produce your taxes. CPAs bill at an hourly rate, the less time it takes them the less money it will cost you to have your taxes prepared.

Get your items to your CPA early – The longer you wait to get your items to your CPA the less time they have to spend on your particular situation. If you wait to the last minute you could get placed on extension, which could mean penalties and interest from the IRS.

Meet with your CPA regularly – Seeing your CPA two to three times a year will keep your CPA relevant in your situation and allow them to properly plan and maximize your benefit. We recommend that everyone meet with his or her CPA every October to produce a tax plan. This will ensure you are taking advantage of any tax credits, deductions, and benefits. It will also ensure that you are not surprised with a big tax bill at the end of the year; and will make sure you are not over withholding for your situation.

The top 6 things you should know about taxes and your money

1. Check your paycheck withholding - even employers make mistakes. Be sure that your withholdings are accurate and add up. Meet with your CPA to make sure your withholdings match your particular situation.

2. Keep your tax records for at least six years in case of an audit

3. If you receive a tax refund, use it to invest in qualified accounts or apply it to future tax bills.

4. Be sure to maximize the benefit of standard deduction vs. itemized deduction

5. Always compare Married Filing Joint vs. Married Filing Separate to ensure the highest refund.

6. Invest long term. Short-term investments are taxed at ordinary rates and can be more volatile than long-term options.

Investment Vehicles

Here are summarized descriptions of some popular investment vehicles. You may be familiar with the ones listed below and that's awesome. I encourage you to continue your education in these areas and most definitely contact and interview 2 to 3 different financial planners/advisers, to assist you in assessing which vehicles best fit your financial situation and future plans.

Traditional IRA

What is a traditional IRA?

A traditional IRA (individual retirement arrangement) is a way to save for retirement, by contributing pre-tax or after-tax dollars to this investment vehicle, you may have immediate tax benefits if your contributions are tax-deductible. Contributions you make to a traditional IRA may be fully or partially deductible, depending on your circumstances and with a Traditional IRA, your money can grow tax-deferred, but you'll pay ordinary income tax on your withdrawals, and you must start taking distributions after age 70½.

Rules and Rewards
- Maximum contributions for 2021
    1. up to age 50: $6000
    2. catch-up age 50 to 70½: $7000
    3. non-income earning spouse: $6000 (in a separate IRA; and the wage earner must earn at least the contributed amount of both IRA's combined)
    4. No contributions can be made after age 70½
- Traditional IRA contribution rules are based on your age, not on income
- Earnings grow tax deferred until your retirement
- When you make withdrawals after age 59½, there are no penalties and you pay ordinary income tax at that time.
- Withdraw before age 59½ and you are subject to a 10% penalty and the current income tax (there are some penalty exceptions which include hardship, medical expenses more than 10% of your AGI, and first time home buyer, rules regarding early distributions from your retirement plan can be complex. Visit the IRS website for

a comprehensive chart of exception. Know your options so you can make an informed decision)

- Contributions to a Traditional IRA may be tax deductible, depending on income level, tax filing and your participation in an employer-sponsored retirement plan.

You're covered by an employer retirement plan for a tax year if your employer (or your spouse's employer) has a:

1. Defined contribution plan (profit-sharing, 401(k), stock bonus and money purchase pension plan) and any contributions or forfeitures were allocated to your account for the plan year ending with or within the tax year
2. Defined benefit plan (pension plan that pays a retirement benefit spelled out in the plan) and you are eligible to participate for the plan year ending with or within the tax year
3. IRA-based plan (SEP, SARSEP or SIMPLE IRA plan) and you had an amount contributed to your IRA for the plan year that ends with or within the tax year

(You can also look at your W2 in Box 13, if it's checked "Retirement plan", you are part of your employer sponsored plan. Check with your HR department for more details)

For more information on IRA'S visit this link to the IRS www.irs.gov/retirement-plans/plan-participant-employee/retirement-topics-contributions also check this IRS pub. : Publication 590-A

The 2020/2021 Traditional IRA income limits and

If you have a retirement plan with your employer

Individual Filer or (head of household)			
2020 MAGI	2020 IRA Contribution Limit	2021 MAGI	2021 IRA Contribution Limit
Less than $65,000	Full	Less than $66,000	Full
$65,000 - $75,000	Partial	$66,000 - $76,000	Partial
$75,000 or more	None	$76,000 or more	None

Married Filing Jointly or qualifying Widow(er)			
2020 MAGI each working	2020 IRA Contribution Limit	2020 MAGI one spouse working & living together	2020 IRA Contribution Limit
Less than $104,000	Full	Less than $196,000	Full
$104,000 - $124,000	Partial	$196,000 - $205,999	Partial
$124,000 or more	None	$206,000 or more	None

Married Filing Separately			
2020 MAGI	2020 IRA Contribution Limit	2021 MAGI	2021 IRA Contribution Limit
$1 - $9,999	Partial	$1 - $9,999	Partial
$10,000 or more	None	$10,000 or more	None

IF YOU DO NOT HAVE a retirement plan through your employer:

Single, Head of household, or Qualifying widow(er): Any modified adjusted gross income (MAGI) permits a full deduction.

Married filing jointly or separately with a spouse who is not covered by a plan at work: Any MAGI permits a full deduction.

Married filing jointly with a spouse who is covered by a plan at work: If your MAGI is $189,000 or less, then you can take a full deduction. If it's more than $189,000, but less than $199,000, then you can take a partial deduction. If it's $199,000 or more, then there is no deduction at all.

Married filing separately with a spouse who is covered by a plan at work: If your MAGI is less than$10,000, then you can claim a partial deduction. If it's $10,000 or more, then there is no deduction.

KnowThis
The deadline to make your yearly IRA contribution is April 15 of the following year.

Roth IRA

A Roth IRA (Individual Retirement Arrangement) is a special type of retirement plan under US law that is generally not taxed, provided certain conditions are met. The tax law of the United States allows a tax reduction on a limited amount of saving for retirement. The Roth IRA's principal difference from most other tax advantaged retirement plans is that, rather than granting a tax break for money placed into the plan, the tax break is granted on the money withdrawn from the plan during retirement.

A Roth IRA can be an individual retirement account containing investments in securities, usually common stocks and bonds, often through mutual funds (although other investments, including derivatives, notes, certificates of deposit, and real estate are possible). A Roth IRA can also be an individual retirement annuity, which is an annuity contract or an endowment contract purchased from a life insurance company.

In contrast to a traditional IRA, contributions to a Roth IRA are not tax-deductible. Withdrawals are generally tax-free, but not always and not without certain stipulations (i.e., tax free for principal withdrawals and the owner's age must be at least 59½ for tax free withdrawals on the growth portion above principal). An advantage of the Roth IRA over a traditional IRA is that there are fewer withdrawal restrictions and requirements. Transactions inside an account (including capital gains, dividends, and interest) do not incur a current tax liability.

Some benefits:

- Assets in the Roth IRA can be passed on to heirs.
- Direct contributions to a Roth IRA may be withdrawn tax free at any time. Rolled-over or converted (before age 59½) contributions held in a Roth IRA may be withdrawn tax and penalty free after the "seasoning" period (currently 5 years). Earnings may be withdrawn tax and penalty free after the seasoning period if the condition of age 59½ (or other qualifying condition) is also met.
- Distributions from a Roth IRA do not increase your Adjusted Gross Income (AGI). This is important because it means that these distributions are income tax free and there is also the benefit of not increasing your marginal

income tax bracket.
- If a Roth IRA owner dies, and his/her spouse becomes the sole beneficiary of that Roth IRA while also owning a separate Roth IRA, the spouse is permitted to combine the two Roth IRAs into a single plan without penalty
- Unlike distributions from a regular IRA, qualified Roth distributions do not affect the calculation of taxable social security benefits.

Some drawbacks

- A taxpayer who pays state income taxes and who contributes to a Roth IRA (instead of a traditional IRA or a tax deductible employer sponsored retirement plan) will have to pay state income taxes on the amount contributed to the Roth IRA in the year the money is earned.
- Contributions to a Roth IRA are not tax deductible
- Congress may change the rules that currently allow for tax free withdrawal of Roth IRA contributions. Therefore, someone who contributes to a traditional IRA is guaranteed to realize an immediate tax benefit, whereas someone who contributes to a Roth IRA must wait for a number of years before realizing the tax benefit and that person assumes the risk that the rules might be changed during the interim. Double taxation.
- The perceived tax benefit may never be realized because one might not live to retirement or much beyond, in which case, the tax structure of a Roth only serves to reduce an estate that may not have been subject to tax. One must live until one's Roth IRA contributions have been withdrawn and exhausted to fully realize the tax benefit. Whereas, with a traditional IRA, tax might never be collected at all.

2020/2021 Roth IRA phase limits

Eligibility to contribute to a Roth IRA phases out at certain income limits. (Congress has limited who can contribute to a Roth IRA based upon income. A taxpayer can contribute the maximum only if their Modified Adjusted Gross Income (MAGI) is below a certain level. Otherwise, a phase-out of allowed contributions runs proportionally throughout the MAGI ranges shown below)

Individual Filer / Married filing separate-not living together			
2020 MAGI	2019 Roth IRA Contribution Limit	2021 MAGI	2021 Roth IRA Contribution Limit
Less than $124,000	Full	Less than $125,000	Full
$124000 - $138,999	Partial	$125,000 - $139,999	Partial
$139,000 or more	None	$140,000 or more	None

Married Filing Jointly			
2020 MAGI	2020 Roth IRA Contribution Limit	2021 MAGI	2021 Roth IRA Contribution Limit
Less than $196,000	Full	Less than $198,000	Full
$196,000 - $205,999	Partial	$198,000 - $207,999	Partial
$206,000 or more	None	$208,000 or more	None

Married Filing Separately (living with)			
2020 MAGI	2018 Roth IRA Contribution Limit	2021 MAGI	2019 Roth IRA Contribution Limit
$1 - $9,999	Partial	$1 - $9,999	Partial
$10,000 or more	None	$10,000 or more	None

The total contributions allowed per year to all IRAs is the lesser of one's taxable compensation (which is not the same as adjusted gross income) and the limit amounts as seen below (this total may be split up between any number of traditional and Roth IRAs. In the case of a married couple, each spouse may contribute the amount listed). Here is how the historical IRA contribution limit has changed in recent years since then:

Years:	Maximum IRA Contribution (age under 50)	Maximum IRA Contribution (age over 50)
2002, 2003, 2004	$3,000	$3,500
2005	$4,000	$4,500
2006, 2007	$4,000	$5,000
2008, 2009, 2010, 2011, 2012	$5,000	$6,000
2013, 2014, 2015, 2016, 2017, 2018	$5,500	$6,500
2019	$6,000	$7,000
2020	$6000	$7000

For example, if one is single, aged 49 or under, and earns $10,000, one can contribute a maximum of $5,000 in 2008. However, if one is single and earns $2,000, one can contribute only a maximum of $2,000 in 2008 ($2,000 is the lesser of $2,000 and $5,000).

NOTE:

Coronavirus-related tax relief. Recent legislation provides for tax-favored withdrawals from IRAs for certain individuals who were impacted by the coronavirus in 2020. See Coronavirus Relief in Publication 590-B, Distributions from Individual Retirement Accounts (IRAs), for more information. Refer to IRS publication 590A for (IRA's) & 560 for small businesses.

IRAs	2021	2020	2019
IRA Contribution Limit	$6,000	$6,000	$6,000
IRA Catch-Up Contributions	1,000	1,000	1,000

Traditional IRA AGI Deduction Phase-out Starting at	2021	2020	2019
Joint Return	105,000	104,000	103,000
Single or Head of Household	66,000	65,000	64,000

SEP	2021	2020	2019
SEP Minimum Compensation	650	600	600
SEP Maximum Contribution	58,000	57,000	56,000
SEP Maximum Compensation	290,000	285,000	280,000

SIMPLE Plans	2021	2020	2019
SIMPLE Maximum Contributions	13,500	13,500	13,000
Catch-up Contributions	3,000	3,000	3,000

401(k), 403 (b), Profit-Sharing Plans, etc.	2021	2020	2019
Annual Compensation	290,000	285,000	280,000
Elective Deferrals	19,500	19,500	19,000
Catch-up Contributions	6,500	6,500	6,000
Defined Contribution Limits	58,000	57,000	56,000
ESOP Limits	1,165,000 230,000	1,150,000 230,000	1,130,000 225,000

Other	2021	2020	2019
HCE Threshold	130,000	130,000	125,000
Defined Benefit Limits	230,000	230,000	225,000
Key Employee	185,000	185,000	180,000
457 Elective Deferrals	19,500	19,500	19,000
Control Employee (board member or officer)	115,000	115,000	110,000
Control Employee (compensation-based)	235,000	230,000	225,000

IRA Tips

- Spousal IRA Contributions: Take Advantage of Spousal IRA Contributions! If you are married, you should become familiar with how spousal IRA contributions work, as a spousal IRA could dramatically boost your family's IRA contributions in a given year if either you or your spouse don't earn qualifying income.

- Self-Employment Income: You may be able to deduct business related expenses, such as, your home office. You can contribute a portion of your income to self-employment retirement accounts, such as a solo 401K, SIMPLE IRA, or SEP IRA.

- Backdoor Roth IRA: if your income is over the Traditional and Roth IRA income limits, a Backdoor Roth IRA could be a smart move (if you follow proper caution).

- Tax Credit for Contributing: If your income is low enough, you might also qualify for the Saver's Credit for contributing to one of these types of retirement accounts.

- If you have old 401K's sitting around from jobs long forgotten, you should consider consolidating your 401K's and rolling over to an IRA. IRA's typically have lower fees associated with them.

- Contribution Deadline: Note that the IRA contribution deadline for the 2021 calendar year is up until the tax deadline next April 15, 2022. And you can begin contributing for 2022 on Jan. 1, 2022.

401k

In the United States, a 401(k) plan is the tax-qualified, defined-contribution pension, an account defined in subsection 401(k) of the Internal Revenue Code. Under the plan, retirement savings contributions are provided (and sometimes proportionately matched) by an employer, deducted from the employee's paycheck before taxation (therefore tax-deferred until withdrawn after retirement or as otherwise permitted by applicable law), and limited to a maximum pre-tax annual contribution of $19,500 (as of 2021).

403b

Employer plans for nonprofit institutions, 457(b) and 401a are plans for governmental employers. These plans may provide total annual contribution of $57,000 (as of 2020) per plan participant, including both employee and employer contributions.

Distribution

Withdrawing money from an employer-sponsored retirement plan or any other tax-deferred retirement plan, before age 59½, is doable but costly. Generally, employees are eligible to take penalty-free distributions at age 59½, but the IRS does not require that employees take distributions until the calendar year that the employee turns 70½. People can take distributions from employer-sponsored plans prior to age 59½, but the IRS will assess a penalty of 10% in addition to the income taxes due.

Be sure to consult your plan documents about the specific kinds of distributions that are allowed in your plan and always consult your tax adviser before taking any action that could trigger a taxable event.

Rollovers

Rollovers maybe necessary if you change employers and are investing in your new employer's plan. Rolling into a new employer's 401(k) plan will not trigger any taxes or penalties. Combining your old account with your new one allows you to easily track and manage your retirement savings since all money will be in the same account.

You can also rollover into an IRA which doesn't trigger any taxes or penalties. But, know that an IRA rollover means an additional account to manage for individuals who have found alternate employment and will invest in the new employer's retirement plan. Here are a few pros to an IRA investment:

- Access to limitless investment options that these individual accounts offer – a typical 401(k) generally offers 10 to 30 investment options,

- A tax situation that is more advantageous for beneficiaries in the event that the account-holder dies
- Less-extreme partial withdrawal penalties – which might make an IRA rollover a better option than leaving the money in a former employer's 401(k) plan for someone recently laid-off who needs to take a partial distribution.

Mutual Funds

What Does Mutual Fund Mean?

Technically a mutual fund is a professionally managed investment fund such as; stocks, bonds, money market instruments, and similar assets (which are collective investment vehicles that are regulated). They are then sold to the general public on a daily basis (this pools money from many investors in order to purchase securities) with the goal of making a profit, which gives a return to the investor.

Mutual funds are operated by money managers, who actively manage a fund's assets in an attempt to produce positive returns for you, the investor. You would typically choose an investment firm that would manage your mutual fund investment portfolio. As an investor, you have the option of allowing the firm to choose and manage your investment funds or based on your own investment knowledge and risk tolerance. You have the opportunity to choose and/or actively manage what you think is the best investment fund combination that will benefit your financial situation and future goals.

KnowThis
Whether you are investing for balanced income, conservative income, growth income, or a combination thereof, all investing will require research, planning, and strategy.

Credit Score

Credit scores are held at the credit bureau. There are three credit bureaus in the U.S., which are Equifax, Experian and Transunion. The creditors (mortgage lenders, banks, credit card companies), the collection agencies and the courts all report your financial activity to these bureaus. These reports include: credit inquiries, loan approvals and terms, payment history; late pays as well as loan defaults. Bankruptcies and financial judgments against you are also reported.

These reports may be pulled by potential lenders before they approve a loan to see your financial habits and ascertain whether you are a safe risk. Yes, you've guessed it, these reports are a vital part of your financial health. It is important that you know what is in your report and be sure to correct any mistakes. The credit report is comprised of several sections that track your financial health. This generally includes, of course,

- Your personal information: (name, address, social security number) be sure this info matches your identity.
- Your creditors information: car loans, credit cards, mortgage(s), student loans and store accounts. Your creditors report all info on a monthly basis; loan amount/ terms, balances, and payments history.
- Collections info: whether you've been bad and just didn't pay, or you forgot about the bill, or you fell on hard times, if your creditor turned it over to a collection agency, it is reported to the bureau. This is not a good look!
- Public record: if you've filed for bankruptcy, have any financial judgments against you or any tax liens, it's reported to the bureau.
- Inquiries: there are different types of inquiries, but your credit score only reflects the credit inquires.

All of this information is reviewed and analyzed by companies like VantageScore Solutions and FICO. They are not credit bureaus. They are analytical companies that study and analyze the credit report, then summarize the findings into a 3 digit number, known as your "FICO score." This score helps lenders determine if they will extend credit to you, how much they will extend to you and at what interest rate. The higher your score the better terms you receive.

KnowThis
The information the three bureaus have in your Credit Report may be different. This is why you may want to pull a report from each bureau. You should know what's in each report and again, be sure to file disputes and correct any errors you find.

Your credit score plays a vital-role in credit approval and credit terms. It could also affect the outcome of job eligibility, housing approval, and other areas where your financial character is considered.

FICO Scores range from 300-850 (some bureaus may use a range of 250-900). Here's a chart that could represent how institutions may view your scores:

Credit Score Ranges

	Poor	Fair	Good	Very Good	Excellent
FICO Score	300 to 579	580 to 669	670 to 739	740 to 799	800 to 850

So, since the FICO Score could have such an impact on your #comeupmove, #newlife, #debtfreeliving, #doingme, #LivingMyBestLife; it is imperative that you know the dynamics of credit scores.

Fixing credit report errors

(the information below can be reviewed on the Fair Trade Commission website)
www.consumer.ftc.gov/articles/0151-disputing-errors-credit-reports

Correcting errors on your credit report requires you to contact the company reporting the information and the bureau receiving the information. The Fair Credit Reporting Act mandates that the reporting company and the credit bureau are responsible for correcting incomplete and inaccurate information that is recorded in your credit report. Be sure to have correct supporting documentation as this lends to a more-timely transaction. You're gonna need to supply some time and patience here.

A few tips:
- Pinpoint the errors
- Collect supporting documents
- Know the facts (dates, amounts, discrepancies, etc.)
- Know if you want a correction or a deletion on the item in question

The bureau has 30 days to investigate your claim. If you are doing mail correspondence be sure to send it certified mail with return receipt requested and only send copied documents NOT the originals.

Each bureau's website for disputes

www.equifax.com/personal/disputes/
www.experian.com
www.transunion.com/credit-disputes/dispute-your-credit

How to Order Your Free Report

What? Free? Yes, free. The Fair Credit Reporting Act requires that Equifax, Experian, and TransUnion provide a free copy of your credit report, once every 12 months, upon your request. With that, these credit reporting companies have established three ways to order your free annual credit report:

1. one website for all 3 bureaus: To order, visit (annualcreditreport.com)
2. toll-free telephone number: you may call 1-877-322-8228, where you can order your free annual report
3. mailing address: go to: (www.consumer.ftc.gov/articles/pdf-0093-annual-report-request-form.pdf) complete the Annual Credit Report Request Form and mail it to: Annual Credit Report Request Service

> P.O. Box 105281
> Atlanta, GA 30348-5281

KnowThis
There are several companies that provide services that assist you in getting your credit reports (for a fee), including the 3 credit bureaus. I encourage you to do a little leg work and take advantage of the free services provided.

Do you have a business mind?

YOU WANT TO START A BUSINESS?

Starting a business involves planning, making key financial decisions, and completing a series of legal activities. I recommend using the resources offered at your state web site which should be: _your state.gov_. When you're there, go to the search box type in <u>one stop business</u>; the resources here will be the info needed to make you official. Also refer to the <u>sba.org</u> website, there are enormous amount of resources offered to assist you in starting and maintaining a successful business at this site. (SBA works with a number of local partners to counsel, mentor, and train small businesses)

Here are a few basic items to consider when getting started with your Business.

1. Do you know any regulations for this business?

Learn about regulations and ordinances that affect your industry and can impact your business

Know your business; research, research, research.

There is some element of risk in every business venture. The entrepreneur's responsibility is to learn all you can about the business you choose to start. This involves exhaustive research, planning and preparation. These steps will provide the necessary tools for making realistic business projections and can minimize the risk factor.

Be sure you know if your business is required to follow any state or local government regulations and ordinances. Requirements could include any of the following; a license, insurance or a permit. A good place to start is your local zoning office and your state's web site (search: _new businesses_). Most states have a one-stop business packet for start-up businesses.

2. Do you have a plan?

Will your business provide a service or a product? Who is your customer or client? What is your mission?… This information will be included in your Business Plan, which is the foundation to the success of your business (of course, God gets all the glory).

You need motivation?.......

Listen, when you commit to starting your own business it can be an intimidating venture, but after you begin researching the necessary components of the business and putting that information in your business plan, you will see your vision, your dream come to life on paper. Understand that a well-researched and well written business plan allows you to see a dream turn into an organization with a mission, with purpose and growth potential.

With a well written business plan you are ready to talk with potential partners and meet with financial institutions. This plan will also provide you with organizational structure, management structure, staff requirements and financial projections.

A business plan can be a guiding light for a company in two ways; first, because it conveys structure and second, it's motivation. For me, regularly referring to my plan keeps me focused and ensures that the business is on course with meeting its goals. Are you motivated?

Here is an outline of the different sections you can include in your plan:

Table of Contents

3. Do You Need Money?

When starting a business, you will want to research the possible need for financing your business. There are generally start-up costs associated with new businesses such as: rental contracts, office equipment, necessary products, advertisement, etc. Even as your business grows there may be a need for financing to cover operating expenses (i.e. utilities, supplies, payroll). This information should be expressed in a well-researched and well-written business plan. Your business plan will be used in securing financing if you choose to seek assistance from a bank or from investors. You should know that banks and investors will want to review your plan to see the plan of operation, what your expense and revenue projections are and to ascertain whether the business will have enough growth and profit to repay a loan. The business plan is a very import tool for the success of the business.

4. Do you have a name?

The Name

If you're not using your personal name for the business, then you will need to choose a business name and register it with the state as a "Doing Business As" (DBA) name. To do business in most states legally you must register with the Secretary of State and the Department of Revenue. When you visit your state website (your state.gov) or your "Secretary of State" website, search for "One Stop Business", most states have consolidated the tools needed for a start-up business in this "One Stop" format to assist you in putting your business on the fast track. (time is money)

NOTE: many cities and counties also require registration for individuals and firms conducting business within their jurisdiction. To learn about your requirements in your area, **consult your local county/city clerks.**

TRADEMARK

Although it is not mandatory to do so, it is very important to register a trade mark for the name of your business as well as for the name(s) of any specific products that you manufacture and / or sell. The reason for this is that a trade mark registration provides an "umbrella" right that entitles the proprietor to prevent the unauthorized use of not only an identical or confusingly similar trade mark, but also an identical or confusingly similar company name, trading name and domain name.

5. Do you know which legal structure you'll use?

Your legal structure

One of the first decisions to make when starting a business is choosing the most appropriate legal structure for your business. There are several important factors to consider when choosing a business structure. Two of the most important questions to answer are:

- How does the structure impact my personal liability for things that happen in the business?
- How does the structure affect the amount of tax I will have to pay?

I believe
It is good and sound business judgment to seek advice from an accountant and/or attorney before starting a business.

Sole Proprietor

Definition: *A sole proprietorship is a business that is owned and operated by a natural person (individual). This is the simplest form of business entity. The sole proprietorship is not a legal entity. The business has no existence separate from the owner who is called the proprietor. – SARS*
Individual status requires no additional filing or record keeping, though the IRS will require you to keep accounting records for tax purposes. The major disadvantage of the sole proprietorship format is personal liability. You have unlimited personal liability for all lawsuits against your business. Personally, you can lose everything you own, if there is a business or legal dispute and you have a judgment entered against you in a lawsuit.

Partnership

Definition: *A partnership is the relationship existing between two or more persons who join to carry on a trade or business. Each person contributes money, property, labor or skill, and expects to share in the profits and losses of the business. – IRS*

Limited partners cannot take part in the day-to-day management of the firm, however. If they do, they risk having the protections of being a limited partner revoked.

Limited Liability Company

Definition: *Limited liability is a type of liability that does not exceed the amount invested in a partnership or limited liability company. The limited liability feature is one of the biggest advantages of investing in publicly listed companies.* – Investopedia

Limited liability companies are a cross between partnerships and corporations. They do not have any legal status under federal law, but state law allows them to provide their owners with substantial limited liability. They can also choose how to be treated for the purposes of filing their income tax returns. Specifically, LLC members can choose to have their businesses treated as an S-corporation or as a partnership. Single member LLCs can choose to be treated as a sole proprietor for income tax purposes.

Corporations

Corporations are separate legal persons under the law. They have a legal identity that is separate and distinct from that of their owners, and owners are not generally held financially responsible for claims against the corporation. Subchapter S corporations are not taxed at the company level; instead, their profits pass through to shareholder returns and are taxed at the shareholder level. S-corporations also have strict limitations on who may be shareholders. You can have no more than 100 shareholders, and they must be residents or citizens of the U.S. C-corporations do not have these restrictions, but they do pay income taxes at the company level, before passing dividends to the investor. This is called "double taxation" and is a disadvantage of C-corporations. C-corporations may be the best choice, however, for those who plan to expand and who want to have the freedom to raise large amounts of capital by issuing stock.

FRANCHISE

Definition: *A franchise in its' simplest form is an agreement by two parties, the franchisor (the original owner) and the franchisee (the investor). It is a license to perform or carry out specific commercial activities under a trade-name or trademark.*

There is usually an entrance fee and a commitment to pay a percentage of your sales revenue and training requirements associated with these transactions. Some benefits of a franchise are: name recognition, tried and tested service or products, corporate advertising and product improvement and ongoing training. the ground work has been completed in most franchises. Choose the right one and you can ride the ship all the way to the bank.

6. Do you have your tax ID numbers?

Federal An Employer Identification Number (EIN) is also known as a Federal Tax Identification Number and is used to identify a business entity. Generally, businesses need an EIN. You may apply by mail, by fax, by phone and now you may apply online. *This is a free service offered by the Internal Revenue Service and you can get your EIN immediately.* (irs.gov)

State

Depending on your industry and business type there may be additional state tax requirements for your business. *(You must check with your state to see if you need a state number or charter.)*

Local

Many cities and counties require a local business license and/or impose an occupational tax or other type of tax on individuals and firms conducting business within their jurisdiction. To learn about your requirements in this area, *consult your local county and city government officials. You can also contact a tax Attorney or CPA.*

7. Do you know the Insurance Requirements?

Unemployment Insurance

If you hire employees your business may be required to register for unemployment insurance to operate in your state. *Check with state and local government officials (Department of Job and Family Services in your state is a good place to start)*

Workers' Compensation

Most states also requires workers' compensation insurance for many employers and they may provide a fee- based insurance service for you. Some states do not sponsor a state-run insurance program. Therefore, it is the employers' responsibility to secure the insurance from a private insurance carrier or self-insure. ***Check with your state government officials.***

Other Forms of Business Insurance

Make sure you adequately protect your business before you open. Call at least 3 reputable insurance companies for coverage quotes.

- Building insurance
- Fire insurance
- Liability insurance
- Umbrella insurance
- Vehicle insurance

8. Do you know if there are Licenses & Permits required?

- **Federal licenses** - If your business is involved in activities supervised and regulated by a federal agency, you may need to obtain a federal license.

- **Operational licenses** - Some states don't have a statewide business license that applies to all businesses, but certain types of businesses are required to have a special license or permit to legally operate. In some cases, more than one license may be required. ***Check with your state officials.***

- **Environmental permits** - Environmental permits are required by federal, state and sometimes local governments to ensure that business and construction minimize potential impacts on human health and the environment. Many environmental programs require that facilities and operators obtain permits or prior authorizations before engaging in certain activities. Check with your state and local environmental/health officials.

- **Local** - Many cities and counties require a local business license. To learn about your requirements in your area, **consult your local county and city government officials.**

- **Local Occupational License Tax Form Database** - Check with your state and local tax authorities. Also consult with a tax professional (a tax attorney or CPA)

Definitions

A

AARP   Formerly known as the American Association of Retired Persons, AARP is the nation's leading organization for people age fifty and older. Founded in 1958 by retired educator Dr. Ethel Percy Andrus, it is a nonprofit, nonpartisan association with a membership of 40 million. It provides information, education, research, advocacy and community services through a nationwide network of local chapters and experienced volunteers. It focuses its work on consumer issues, economic security, work, health and independent living issues, and engages in legislative, judicial and consumer advocacy in these areas.

APR   Annual percentage rate; it basically is how much it cost you to borrow money. You generally encounter APR's when you're dealing in credit; mortgages, car loans, credit cards. These rates could include fees associated with the loan (you could opt to pay fees upfront if your plan and finances agree, it may save you money long term). There is a fixed APR (it doesn't change during the life of the loan). There are Variable APR's (can change rates and are tied to an index interest whelming the rate, such as prime rate...so if the prime rate change so would a variable rate).. Generally you may want to stay away from debt with high APRs, the could end up overwhelming your plan.

AGI   Adjusted gross income; its your total gross income minus your specific deductions (this is the money you can put in your account). This is what's used to calculate taxable income. This is also the number generally asked for when applying for credit.

ABUSIVE TAX SHELTER   An investment scheme that claims to reduce income tax without changing the value of the user's income or assets. Abusive tax shelters serve no economic purpose other than lowering the federal or state tax owed when filing. Often, these schemes channel funds through trusts or partnerships to avoid taxation.

ABSTRACT OF TITLE   A brief history of the titles for a piece of land. The abstract of title lists all of the legal actions that have been performed or used in conjunction with a piece of property. This is used to determine whether or not there is any kind of claim against a property.

ACCELERATED AMORTIZATION   Extra payments made towards paying down a mortgage principal. With accelerated amortization, the loan borrower is allowed to add additional payments to their mortgage bill in order to pay off a mortgage before the loan settlement date. The benefit of doing so is reduced overall interest payments.

ACCIDENTAL DEATH BENEFIT   The accidental death benefit is payment due to the beneficiary of an accidental death insurance policy, which is often a clause or rider connected to a life insurance policy. The accidental death benefit is usually an amount paid in addition to the standard benefit payable if the insured died of natural causes.

B

BABY BOOMER   Baby boomer is a person who was born between 1946 and 1964. The baby boomer generation makes up a substantial portion of the world's population: it represents nearly 20% of the American public. Baby boomers have had, and continue to have a significant impact on the economy. As a result, they are often the focus of marketing campaigns and business plans.

BAD CHECK   A check drawn on a nonexistent account or on an account with insufficient funds to honor the check when presented.

BAD CREDIT   Bad credit describes an individual's credit history when it indicates that the borrower has a high credit risk. A low credit score signals bad credit, while a high credit score is an indicator of good credit. Creditors who lend money to an individual with bad credit face a greater risk of that individual missing payments or defaulting than creditors who lend to individuals with good credit.

BAD DEBT   is debt that is not collectible and therefore worthless to the creditor. Bad debt is usually a product of the debtor going into bankruptcy but may also occur when the creditor's cost of pursuing the debt collection activities is more than the amount of the debt. Once a debt is considered bad, the business may be able to write it off as an expense on its income tax return.

"Passing" bad checks is illegal, and the crime can range from a misdemeanor to a felony, depending on the amounts involved and whether the activity involved crossing state lines

BALANCE SHEET   A balance sheet is a financial statement that summarizes a company's assets, liabilities and shareholders' equity at a specific point in time. These three balance sheet segments give investors an idea as to what the company owns and owes, as well as the amount invested by shareholders. The balance sheet adheres to the following formula: Assets = Liabilities + Shareholders' Equity

BALANCE TRANFER FEES   A fee levied by a credit card issuer when a balance is transferred to its credit card. A balance transfer fee can range from a low of 1% to as high as 5% of the transferred amount. Balance transfer fees generally go hand-in-hand with special "teaser" interest rates that can be as low as zero percent, but that are only applicable for a period that is usually six to 12 months, after which time interest rates on any outstanding card balance will revert to the usual levels.

A balance transfer fee may be worth paying if you have high levels of credit card debt. Here you may have a case where the upfront cost may be more but is offset by the savings on credit card interest expense.

BANK CARD   Any card issued against a depositary account, such as an ATM card or a debit card. Withdrawals or payments with bank cards will typically result in an immediate corresponding change in the balance of the account on which it is issued.

Bank cards may be limited in their use, Some can only be used at ATM machines or for certain purchases.

BEAR MARKET A bear market is a condition in which securities prices fall and widespread pessimism causes the stock market's downward spiral to be self-sustaining. Although figures vary, a downturn of 20% or more from a peak in multiple broad market indexes, such as the Dow Jones Industrial Average (DJIA) or Standard & Poor's 500 Index (S&P 500), over a two-month period is considered an entry into a bear market.

BEAR A bear is an investor who believes that a particular security or market is headed downward and attempts to profit from a decline in prices. Bears are generally pessimistic about the state of a given market. For example, if an investor were bearish on the Standard & Poor's (S&P) 500, he would attempt to profit from a decline in the broad MARKET INDEX.

BENEFICIARY A beneficiary is any person who gains an advantage and/or profits from something. In the financial world, a beneficiary typically refers to someone who is eligible to receive distributions from a trust, will or life insurance policy. Beneficiaries are either named specifically in these documents or have met the stipulations that make them eligible for whatever distribution is specified.

BITCOIN Bitcoin is a digital currency created in 2009. It follows the ideas set out in a white paper by the mysterious Satoshi Nakamoto, whose true identity has yet to be verified. Bitcoin offers the promise of lower transaction fees than traditional online payment mechanisms and is operated by a decentralized authority, unlike government-issued currencies.

There are no physical bitcoins, only balances kept on a public ledger in the cloud, that – along with all Bitcoin transactions – is verified by a massive amount of computing power.

BLOOMBERG Bloomberg is a major global provider of 24-hour financial news and information, including real-time and historic price data, financials data, trading news and analyst coverage, as well as general news and sports. Its services, which span its own platform, television, radio and magazines, offer professionals analytic tools.

BOND FUND A bond fund is a fund invested primarily in bonds and other debt instruments. The exact type of debt the fund invests in will depend on its focus, but investments may include government, corporate, municipal and convertible bonds, in addition to other debt securities like mortgage-backed securities (MBS).A bond fund Can also be referred to as a debt fund.

BROKER

1. A broker is an individual or firm that charges a fee or commission for executing buy and sell orders submitted by an investor.

2. The role of a firm when it acts as an agent for a customer and charges the customer a commission for its services.

3. A licensed real estate professional who typically represents the seller of a property. A broker's duties may include; determining, advertising properties for sale, showing properties to prospective buyers, and advising clients with regard to offers and related matters.

BULL A bull is an investor who thinks the market, a specific security or an industry is poised to rise. Investors who takes a bull approach purchases securities under the assumption that he can sell them later at a higher price. Bulls are optimistic investors who are presently predicting good things for the market and are attempting to profit from this upward movement.

BULL MARKET A bull market is a financial market of a group of securities in which prices are rising or are expected to rise. The term "bull market" is most often used to refer to the stock market but can be applied to anything that is traded, such as bonds, currencies and commodities.

BUSINESS MODEL A business model is a company's plan for how it will generate revenues and make a profit. It explains what products or services the business plans to manufacture and market, and how it plans to do so, including what expenses it will incur.

C

C CORPRATION   A c corporation is a legal structure that businesses can choose to organize themselves under to limit their owners' legal and financial liabilities. C corporations are an alternative to S corporations, where profits pass through to owners and are only taxed at the individual level, and limited liability companies, which provide the legal protections of corporations but are taxed like sole proprietorships

CAPITAL   Capital refers to financial assets or the financial value of assets, such as funds held in deposit accounts, as well as the tangible machinery and production equipment used in environments such as factories and other manufacturing facilities. Other examples include automobiles, patents, software and brand names. All of these items are inputs that can be used to create wealth.

CAPITAL GAINES TAX   A capital gains tax is a type of tax levied on capital gains, which are profits an investor realizes when he sells a capital asset for a price that is higher than the purchase price.

CHAPTER 11   Chapter 11 is a form of bankruptcy that involves a reorganization of a debtor's business affairs, debts and assets. Named after the U.S. bankruptcy code 11, Chapter 11 is generally filed by corporations that require time to restructure their debts, and it gives the debtor a fresh start, subject to the debtor's fulfillment of his obligations under the plan of reorganization. As the most complex of all bankruptcy cases and generally the most expensive, a company should consider Chapter 11 reorganization only after careful analysis and exploration of all other alternatives.

CHAPTER 13   A U.S. bankruptcy proceeding in which the debtor undertakes a reorganization of his or her finances under the supervision and approval of the courts. As part of the reorganization, the debtor must submit and follow through with a plan to repay outstanding creditors within three to five years. In most circumstances, the repayment plan must provide a substantial payback to creditors - at least equal to what they would receive under other forms of bankruptcy - and it must, if needed, use 100% of the debtor's income for repayment.

CHAPTER 7   Chapter 7 is a bankruptcy proceeding in which a company stops all operations and goes completely out of business. A trustee is appointed to liquidate (sell) the company's assets, the proceeds are used to pay off the debts, and then the remaining debt is discharged. Individuals may declare Chapter 7 bankruptcy as well.

CLEAR TITLE   Also known as "clean title," "just title," "good title" and "free and clear title." A clear title is a title without any kind of lien or levy from creditors or other parties and poses no question as to legal ownership. For example, an owner of a car with a clear title is the sole undisputed owner, and no other party can make any kind of legal claim to its ownership

CLOSED END FUND   A closed-end fund is organized as a publicly traded investment company by the Securities and Exchange Commission (SEC). Like a mutual fund, a closed-end fund is a pooled investment fund with a manager overseeing the portfolio; it raises a fixed amount of capital through an initial public offering (IPO). The fund is then structured, listed and traded like a stock on a stock exchange.

CLOSING

1. The end of a trading session. The closing of a trading day halts trading on exchanges. After-hours trading still occurs until 8 pm.

2. An action which will eliminate your position in a security. Closing a position is done by taking an action which will take away your exposure to risk.

3. The final procedure in a sale in which documents are signed and recorded. This is the time when the ownership of the property is transferred.

CLOSING COST   Closing costs are the expenses, over and above the price of the property, that buyers and sellers normally incur to complete a real estate transaction. Costs incurred may include loan origination fees, discount points, appraisal fees, title searches, title insurance, surveys, taxes, deed-recording fees and credit report charges. Prepaid costs are those that recur over time, such as property taxes and homeowners' insurance. The lender is required by law to state these costs in a "good faith estimate" within three days of a home loan application.

COLLATERAL   Collateral is a property or other asset that a borrower offers as a way for a lender to secure the loan. If the borrower stops making the promised loan payments, the lender can seize the collateral to recoup its losses. Since collateral offers some security to the lender should the borrower fail to pay back the loan, loans that are secured by collateral typically have lower interest rates than unsecured loans. A lender's claim to a borrower's collateral is called a lien.

COMMISION   A commission is a service charge assessed by a broker or investment advisor in return for providing investment advice and/or handling the purchase or sale of a security. Most major, full-service brokerages derive much of their profits from charging commissions on client transactions. Commissions vary widely from brokerage to brokerage.

COMMODITY   A raw material or primary agricultural product that can be bought and sold, such as copper or coffee.

COMMODITY TRADER   A commodity trader focuses on investing in physical substances like oil and gold. Most often these traders are dealing in raw materials used at the beginning of the production value chain such as copper for construction or grains for animal feed. These traders take positions based on forecasted economic trends or arbitrage opportunities in the commodity markets. Oil and gold are two of the most common traded commodities, but markets exist for cotton, wheat, sugar, cattle, pork bellies, lumber, silver and other precious metals.

COMMON STOCK   Common stock is a security that represents ownership in a corporation. Holders of common stock exercise control by electing a board of directors and voting on corporate policy. Common stockholders are on the bottom of the priority ladder for ownership structure; in the event of liquidation, common shareholders have rights to a company's assets only after bondholders, preferred shareholders and other debtholders are paid in full.

COMPOUND INTEREST   Compound interest (or compounding interest) is interest calculated on the initial principal and also on the accumulated interest of previous periods of a deposit or loan. Thought to have originated in 17th-century Italy, compound interest can be thought of as "interest on interest," and will make a sum grow at a faster rate than simple interest, which is calculated only on the principal amount. The rate at which compound interest accrues depends on the frequency of compounding; the higher the number of compounding periods, the greater the compound interest. Thus, the amount of compound interest accrued on $100 compounded at 10% annually will be lower than that on $100 compounded at 5% semi-annually over the same time period. *(Compound interest is calculated by multiplying the principal amount by one plus the annual interest rate raised to the number of compound periods minus one. The total initial amount of the loan is then subtracted from the resulting value.)*

CONDUIT IRA   A traditional IRA that holds only assets that were distributed from a qualified plan. Typically, the intention of using this type of plan is to store assets until they can be rolled into a new employer's qualified plan. *(Should any other assets be commingled with the assets in a conduit IRA, the IRA will lose its conduit status and the assets are no longer eligible for capital gains and forward averaging tax treatments. There is no limit on the contributions transferred to a conduit IRA.)*

CONSUMER CREDIT   Consumer credit is a debt that a person incurs when purchasing a good or service. Consumer credit includes purchases obtained with credit cards, lines of credit and some loans. Consumer credit is also known as consumer debt.

Consumer credit is divided into two classifications: revolving credit and installment credit. The most common form of consumer credit is a credit card.

CONTINGENCY   Contingency is a potential negative event which may occur in the future such as a natural disaster, fraudulent activity or a terrorist attack. In finance, managers often attempt to identify and plan for any contingencies that they feel may occur with any significant likelihood. To mitigate risk, financial managers often err on the conservative side, assuming slightly worse-than-expected outcomes, and arranging a company's affairs so that it can weather negative outcomes with the least distress possible.

COOLING-OFF RULE   A term referring to law pertaining to newly-entered contracts that allows both sides of the party a period of time (after the contract has been signed) to release themselves from any obligations without penalty. (Different types of transactions will have different cooling-off rules, and not all types of contracts have such provisions. Typically this period will be three days; however, it is imperative that all the rules and regulations listed in the fine print are read before entry into a contract.)

COUNTER OFFER   An offer that provides new terms or conditions becomes a counteroffer. However, the offer may limit, change, or add some or all the terms of the original offer.

A counteroffer is a proposal that is made as a result of an undesirable offer. A counteroffer revises the initial offer and makes it more desirable for the person making the new offer. This type of offer permits a person to decline a previous offer and allows offer negotiations to continue.

CREDIT HISTORY   A record of a consumer's ability to repay debts and demonstrated responsibility in repaying debts. A consumer's credit history consists of information such as: number and types of credit accounts, how long each account has been open, amounts owed, amount of available credit used, whether bills are paid on time, and number of recent credit inquiries. It also contains information regarding whether the consumer has any bankruptcies, liens, judgments or collections. This information is all contained on a consumer's credit report.

CREDIT REPAIR   Credit repair is the process of fixing poor credit standing that may have deteriorated for a variety of different reasons. Repairing credit standing may be as simple as disputing mistakes information with the credit agencies. Identity theft, and they damage incurred, may require extensive credit repair work. Another form of credit repair is to deal with fundamental financial issues, such as budgeting, and begin to address legitimate concerns on the part of lenders. *(Individuals are entitled to free credit reports every 12 months from credit reporting agencies, as well as when an adverse action is taken against them, such as being denied credit based on information in the report.)*

CREDIT REPORT   A credit report is a detailed report of an individual's credit history. Credit bureaus collect information and create credit reports based on that information, and lenders use the reports along with other details to determine loan applicants' credit worthiness. In the United States, there are three major credit reporting bureaus: Equifax, Experian and TransUnion. Each of these reporting companies collects information about consumers' personal details and their bill-paying habits to create a unique credit report; although most of the information is similar, there are often small differences between the three reports. *(The Fair Credit Reporting Act requires each of the three credit reporting bureaus to supply consumers with a free credit report once per year.)*

CREDIT SCORE   A credit score is a statistical number that evaluates a consumer's creditworthiness and is based on credit history. Lenders use credit scores to evaluate the probability that an individual will repay his or her debts. A person's credit score ranges from 300 to 850, and the higher the score, the more financially trustworthy a person is considered to be

(Consumers can possess high scores by maintaining a long history of paying their bills on time and keeping their debt low.)

D

DAY TRADER   A day trader engages in long and short trades in an attempt to profit by capitalizing on the intraday movements of a market's price action resulting from temporary inefficiencies in the supply and demand of the moment. A day trader often closes out all trades before the market close and does not hold any open positions overnight. Some day traders use leverage to magnify the returns generated from small stock price movements

DEBT-TO-INCOME RATIO - 'DTI'   The debt-to-income (DTI) ratio is a personal finance measure that compares an individual's debt payment to his or her overall income. The debt-to-income ratio is one way lenders, including mortgage lenders, measure an individual's ability to manage monthly payment and repay debts. DTI is calculated by dividing total recurring monthly debt by gross monthly income, and it is expressed as a percentage. *(A low debt-to -income (DTI) ratio demonstrates a good balance between debt and income. Borrowers who have lower DTIs are more likely to successfully manage monthly debt payments, so lenders prefer to see low numbers. In general, 43% is the highest DTI a borrower can have and still get qualified for a mortgage. A debt-to-income ratio smaller than 36%, however, is preferable, with no more than 28% of that debt going towards servicing a mortgage.)*

DEED A legal document that grants the bearer a right or privilege, provided that he or she meets a number of conditions. In order to receive the privilege - usually ownership, the bearer must be able to do so without causing others undue hardship. A person who poses a risk to society as a result of holding a deed may be restricted in his or her ability to use the property.

Deeds are most known for being used to transfer the ownership of automobiles or land between two parties.

DEED IN LIEU OF FORCLOSURE A potential option taken by a mortgagor (a borrower) to avoid foreclosure under which the mortgagor deeds the collateral property (the home) back to the mortgagee (the lender) in exchange for the release of all obligations under the mortgage. Both sides must enter into the agreement voluntarily and in good faith. *(A deed in lieu of foreclosure has advantages for both a borrower and a lender; mainly the avoidance of time consuming and costly foreclosure proceedings. In addition, the borrower avoids some public notoriety, and may even be able to lease the property back from the lender. The lender needs to assess certain risks which include, among other things, the risk that the property is not worth more than the remaining balance on the mortgage and that junior creditors might hold liens on the property.)*

DISCOUNT RATE   The discount rate is the interest rate charged to commercial banks and other depository institutions for loans received from the Federal Reserve's discount window. The discount rate also refers to the interest rate used in discounted cash flow analysis to determine the present value of future cash flows.

DISCOUNT POINTS   Discount points are a type of prepaid interest or fees mortgage borrowers can purchase that lowers the amount of interest they have to pay on subsequent payments. Each discount point generally costs 1% of the total loan amount and depending on the borrower, each point lowers the loan's interest rate by one-eighth to one one-quarter of a percent. Discount points are tax deductible only for the year in which they were paid. *(Discount points are also known as mortgage points. They are a one-time, upfront mortgage closing cost which five a mortgage borrower access to discounted mortgage rates as compared to the market. Because the IRS considers discount points to be prepaid mortgage interest, they are tax deductible only for the year in which they were paid.)*

DIVERSIFIED FUND   A diversified fund is a fund that is broadly diversified across multiple market sectors or geographic regions. It holds multiple securities, often in multiple asset classes. Its broad market diversification helps to prevent idiosyncratic events in one area from affecting an entire portfolio. *(A diversified fund contrasts with specialized or focused funds, such as sector funds, which focus on stocks in specific sectors such as biotechnology, pharmaceuticals or utilities.)*

DOUBLE NET LEASE   A double net lease is a lease agreement in which the tenant is responsible for both property taxes and premiums for insuring the building. Unlike a single net lease, which only requires the tenant to pay property taxes, a double net lease passes more expenses along in the form of insurance payments. The landlord is still held responsible for structural maintenance expenses. Each month, the landlord receives the base rent plus the additional payments.

DRY CLOSING   A dry closing is a type of real estate closing in which the entire closing requirements are fulfilled except the disbursement of funds. In a dry closing, all involved parties agree that the closing can still happen, and the funds are transferred as soon as possible following the closing. A real estate closing is the completion of a transaction involving the sale or exchange or real estate. In a traditional closing, the title to the property is transferred to the purchaser and all finances pertaining to the purchase are settled.

DUN & BRADSTREET (D&B)   Dun & Bradstreet is a corporation that offers information on commercial credit as well as reports on businesses. Most notably, Dun & Bradstreet is recognizable for its Data Universal Numbering System (D.U.N.S.) numbers; these generate business information reports for more than 100 million companies around the globe.

DUNS NUMBER   A data universal numbering system (DUNS) number is a nine-digit number that uniquely identifies a business. Dun & Bradstreet (D&B) created the number, which generates a business profile in its database that provides the name of a company, phone number, address, number of workers and line of work, along with other relevant information about the company. *(The numbering system was created by Dun & Bradstreet (D&B) in 1983 to identify businesses for data processing and to support its business credit reporting system. In October 1994, it was adopted as the standard business identifier for federal government electronic commerce.)*

E

EARLY WITHDRAWAL   The removal of funds from a fixed-term investment before the maturity date, or the removal of funds from a tax-deferred investment account or retirement savings account, such as an IRA or 401(k) before a prescribed time. Early withdrawal could be anything earlier than the account owner's attainment of a prescribed minimum age requirement, or the maturity of a fixed-term investment, such as a certificate of deposit (CD). When an early withdrawal is made, the investor usually incurs an early withdrawal fee, which acts as a deterrent to frequent withdrawals before the end of the early withdrawal period

EARNED INCOME   Earned income is income derived from active participation in a trade or business, including wages, salary, tips, commissions and bonuses. Earned income includes any income that a person or company receives for work they have done – AKA "personal efforts". If you collect regular dividends from a stock, or receive a monetary gift, that money would be considered unearned income because you didn't do anything to earn it.

EASEMENT   Easement is a real estate concept that defines a scenario in which one party uses the property of another party, where a fee is paid to the owner of the property in return for the right of easement. Easements are often purchased by public utility companies for the right to erect telephone poles or run pipes either above or beneath private property. However, while fees are paid to the property owner, easements can negatively affect property values in that unsightly power lines, for example, can lower the visual appeal of a piece of land.

EDUCATION CREDIT   A type of tax credit available to students of a post-secondary educational institution, such as a college or university. Education credits may be claimed by those who incur qualifying educational expenses, such as tuition and fees. Parents who pay these expenses for their children may be able to claim this type of credit on their tax returns, subject to certain income restrictions. *(There are two types of education credits, the Hope Credit and the Lifetime Learning Credit. The Hope Credit applies to first and second year postsecondary students, with certain restrictions. The*

Lifetime Learning Credit applies to all students at the undergraduate or graduate level. You cannot claim both the Hope and Lifetime Learning Credits for the same student in the same year)

EDUCATION IRA   A savings plan for higher education. Parents and guardians are allowed to make nondeductible contributions to an education IRA or a child under the age of 18. The education IRA is now referred to as the Coverdell ESA. The funds in an education IRA can be withdrawn tax free when they are needed for educational purposes.

ELDERLY and DISABLED CREDIT   A non-refundable tax credit available for taxpayers who are aged 65 or over, or who are permanently and totally disabled. The Elderly and Disabled Credit is designed to provide a measure of financial relief for low-income senior citizens and taxpayers who are unable to engage in any kind of gainful employment as a result of their disability. *(The Elderly and Disabled Credit is claimed on Schedule R of the 1040, or part 3 of the 1040A. Married couples must file jointly to claim the credit, and income and Social Security benefit limitations also apply. A physician must certify that the taxpayer meets the IRS' criteria for disability in writing the first year that the credit is claimed.)*

ESTATE PLANNING   Estate planning is the collection of preparation tasks that serve to manage an individual's asset base in the event of their incapacitation or death, including the bequest of assets to heirs and the settlement of estate taxes. Most estate plans are set up with the help of an attorney experienced in estate law.

Some of the major estate planning tasks include:

- *Creating a will*
- *Limiting estate taxes by setting up trust accounts in the name of beneficiaries*
- *Establishing a guardian for living dependents*
- *Naming an executor of the estate to oversee the terms of the will*
- *Creating/updating beneficiaries on plans such as life*

insurance, IRAs and 401(k)s

- *Setting up funeral arrangements*
- *Establishing annual gifting to reduce the taxable estate*
- *Setting up durable power of attorney (POA) to direct other assets and investment*

(Estate planning is an ongoing process and should be started as soon as one has any measurable asset base.)

ENTREPRENEUR An entrepreneur is an individual who, rather than working as an employee, founds and runs a small business, assuming all the risks and rewards of the venture. The entrepreneur is commonly seen as an innovator, a source of new ideas, goods, services and business/or procedures. Entrepreneurs play a key role in any economy. These are the people who have the skills and initiative necessary to anticipate current and future needs and bring good new ideas to market.

ESTATE TAX A estate tax is levied on an heir's inherited portion of an estate if the value of the estate exceeds an exclusion limit set by law. The estate tax is mostly imposed on assets left to heirs, but it does not apply to the transfer of assets to a surviving spouse. The right of spouses to leave any amount to one another is known as the unlimited marital deduction, but when the surviving spouse who inherited an estate dies, the beneficiaries may then owe estate taxes if the estate exceeds the exclusion limit.

F

FEDERAL DEPOSIT INSURANCE CORPORATION (FDIC) The Federal Deposit Insurance Corporation (FDIC) is an independent federal agency insuring deposits in U.S. banks and thrifts in the event of bank failures. The FDIC was created in 1933 to maintain public confidence and encourage stability in the financial system through the promotion of sound banking practices. As of 2016, the FDIC insures deposits up to$250,000 per depositor as long as the institution is a member firm.

FACE VALUE   Face value is the nominal value or dollar value of a security stated by the issuer. For stocks, it is the original cost of the stock shown on the certificate. For bonds, it is the amount paid to the holder at maturity, generally $1,000. It is also known as "par value" or simply "par."

FAIR HOUSING ACT   The Fair Housing Act (Title VIII of the Civil Rights Act of 1968) prohibits discrimination in the buying, selling, rental or financing of housing based on race, skin color, sex, nationality, religion or any other protected class characteristics. Protections for persons with disabilities and/or children were added to the Fair Housing Act in 1988.

FAMILY AND MEDICAL LEAVE ACT (FMLA)   The Family and Medical Leave Act (FMLA) was signed into law on August 5, 1993 by President Bill Clinton. The FMLA is a labor law requiring larger employers to provide employees unpaid leave for serious health conditions, to care for a sick family member, or to care for a newborn or adopted child. *(An employee who takes unpaid leave that falls under the FMLA is job-protected; that is, the employee can return to the same position held before the leave began. If the same position is unavailable, the employer must provide a position that is substantially equal in pay, benefits and responsibility. To qualify for FMLA, an employee must be employed by a business with 50 or more employees within a 75 mile radius of his or her work site.)*

FEDERAL DIRECT LOAN PROGRAM   The Federal Direct Loan Program is a program that provides low-interest loans to postsecondary students and their parents. The William D. Ford Federal Direct Loan Program is issued and managed by the U.S. Department of Education and is the only government-backed student loan program in the United States. Students who wish to apply for funding must first submit the Free Application for Federal Student Aid (FAFSA).

FEDERAL HOUSING ADMINISTRATION   The Federal Housing Administration (FHA) is a U.S. agency that offers mortgage insurance to lenders that are FHA-approved and meet specified qualifications. Such insurance allows for the protection of lenders against losses that may arise with mortgage defaults. If a borrower defaults on a loan, the FHA pays the lender a specified claim amount. *(The FHA was established with the primary goal of stimulating the housing industry. The underlying idea was that by providing insurance to lending parties, more individuals/customers would qualify for mortgages and be able, or more able, to buy homes.)*

FHA 203(k) LOAN   An FHA 203(k) loan is a type of government -insured mortgage that allows the borrower to take out one loan for two purposes – home purchase and home renovation. An FHA 203 (k) loan is wrapped around rehabilitation or repairs to a home that will become the mortgagor's primary residence. Also known as FHA Construction Loan.

FICO (FAIR ISAAC)   A major analytics software company that provides products and services to both businesses and consumers. The Fair Isaac Corporation, more commonly known as FICO, is best known for producing the most widely used consumer credit scores that financial institutions use in deciding whether to lend money or issue credit. Fair Isaac has offices in 25 locations worldwide, mainly in the United States, Europe and Asia, and its clients include hundreds of banks, insurance companies and retailers. Fair Isaac also provides collections and recovery consulting, customer strategy consulting, operational readiness reviews and other services to businesses *(Fair Isaac was founded in 1956 by engineer Bill Fair and mathematician Earl Isaac. Today, the company holds more than 130 patents for its technologies. Because FICO gives businesses a convenient way to assess consumers' credit risk through FICO scoring, consumers have greater access to credit.)*

FICO SCORE   A FICO score is a type of credit score created by the Fair Isaac Corporation. Lenders use borrowers' FICO scores along with other details on borrowers' credit reports to assess credit risk and determine whether to extend credit. FICO scores take into account various factors in five areas to determine credit worthiness: payment history, current level of indebtedness, types of credit used, length of credit history and new credit accounts. *(FICO* *scores range between 300 and 850. In general, scores above 650 indicate a very good credit history.)*

FIDUCIARY   Essentially, a fiduciary is a person or organization that owes to another the duties of good faith and trust. The highest legal duty of one party to another, it also involves being bound ethically to act in the other's best interests. A fiduciary might be responsible for general well-being, but often it involves finances – managing the assets of another person, or of a group of people, for example. Money managers, bankers, accountants, executors, board members, and corporate officers can all be considered fiduciaries.

FIRST-TIME HOME BUYER   An individual who is purchasing a principal residence for the first time. First-time home buyers are more commonly recognized according to several criteria with regards to an individual retirement account (IRA). If these criteria are met the owner can be granted special privileges, such as exemption from the early-distribution penalty. *(The purchase does not need to be a traditional home in order for the individual to qualify as a first-time homebuyer, but it must be the principal residence.)*

FIVE C"s OF CREDIT   The five C's of credit is a system used by lenders to gauge the creditworthiness of potential borrowers. The system weighs five characteristics of the borrower and conditions of the loan, attempting to estimate the chance of default. The five C's of credit are character, capacity, capital, collateral and conditions. *(The five C's of credit method of evaluating a borrower incorporates both qualitative and quantitative measures. Lenders look at a borrower's credit reports, credit score, income statements and other documents relevant to the borrower's financial situation, and they also consider information about the loan itself.)*

FIVE-YEAR RULE   If a retirement account owner dies before the required beginning date for receiving distributions, the beneficiary may distribute the inherited assets over his/her (the beneficiary's) life expectancy or distribute the assets under the five-year rule. Under the five-year rule, the assets must be distributed by December 31 of the fifth year since the retirement account owner's death. *(The five-year rule does not apply if the IRA owner dies after the required beginning date (RBD).)*

FIXED INTEREST RATE   A fixed interest rate is an interest rate on a liability, such as a loan or mortgage, that remains the same either for the entire term of the loan or for part of the term. A fixed interest rate is attractive to borrowers who do not want their interest rates to rise over the term of their loans, increasing their interest expenses. *(A fixed interest rate avoids the interest rate risk that comes with a floating or variable interest rate,)*

FLIPPING   Flipping refers to purchasing an asset with the intent of selling it for a quick profit rather than holding on for long-term appreciation. Flipping is used to describe short term real estate transactions as well as the activities of some investors in initial public offerings (IPO). Although these are the most common uses in finance, flipping can be used to describe the purchase of any asset that is meant to be sold in the near-term for a profit, including cars, cryptocurrencies, concert tickets and so on.

FORBES   Forbes is an American media and publishing company headed by former Republican candidate Steve Forbes. Perhaps best known for Forbes Magazine, the financial media giant holds ownership positions in Realclearmarkets.com, Realclearsports.com and Realclearpolitics.com. *(Forbes provides daily new coverage on business, technology, financial markets, personal finance, sports and a wide array of other topics.)*

FORECLOSURE   Foreclosure is the legal process through which a lender seizes a property, evicts the homeowner and sells the home after a homeowner is unable to make full principal and interest payments on his or her mortgage, as stipulated in the mortgage contract. *(The foreclosure process derives its legal basis from a mortgage or deed of trust contract, which give the lender the right to use a property as collateral in case the buyer fails to uphold his or her repayment obligation.)*

FORM 1095-A   An IRS form sent to anybody who received health insurance coverage through a Health Insurance Marketplace. The form shows such information as the effective date of the coverage, premium amounts, and any advance payments of the premium tax credit or subsidy. *(Your health insurance coverage now affects your taxes. You may be eligible for a tax credit, or if you failed to have health insurance coverage throughout the year, you may owe a substantial tax penalty (see Obamacare Penalty Enforcement: How It Works).*

FORM 8857: REQUEST FOR INNOCENT SPOUSE RELIEF   An IRS tax form used by taxpayers to request relief from a tax liability involving a spouse or former spouse. Couples filing a joint tax return both become responsible for the tax obligation, called joint and several liability. If additional tax has to be paid because of income, deductions or credits from one spouse (or former spouse), the other partner will still be liable. The taxpayer seeking relief should file Form 8857 as soon as he or she becomes aware of a tax obligation that the other spouse (or former spouse) should be solely responsible for. *(Getting a divorce doesn't stop the IRS from considering both parties still joint and severally liable for a tax obligation, even if a divorce decree states that only one party is responsible for the tax.)*

Form 1310: Statement Of Person Claiming Refund Due A Deceased Taxpayer   A tax form distributed by the Internal Revenue Service (IRS) and used by taxpayers looking to claim a refund on behalf of a deceased person. Form 1310 should be used unless the filer is a surviving spouse submitting a joint return, or if the filer is a personal representative filing an original Form 1040 for the deceased - in which case a court certificate must be attached indicating the appointment of the personal representative. *(Form 1310 is used to match the taxpayer claiming the refund with the deceased. It also provides information on whether a will was left.)*

G

G.I. BILL   The informal name of a United States law that gives military veterans a variety of benefits, including business loans, mortgages, education-expense assistance and unemployment payments. The G.I. Bill, formally called the Servicemen's Readjustment Act of 1944, provided these benefits to men and women following WWII.

(The G.I. Bill is considered one of the most significant pieces of 20th century legislation passed by the U.S. Congress.)

GAME CHANGER   1. A person who is a visionary. 2. A company that alters its business strategy and conceives an entirely new business plan. This type of company switches up and forms a new business strategy in order to compete directly or indirectly with competitors. A game changer changes the way that something is done, thought about or made. *(Game changers are people or organizations that see a new way to complete a task that is more efficient than the traditional methods. THIS SOUNDS LIKE YOU.)*

GARNISHMENT   Garnishment refers to a legal process that instructs a third party to deduct payments directly from a debtor's wage or bank account. Typically, the third party is the debtor's employer and is known as the garnishee. Federal law prohibits employers from firing a worker to avoid processing a garnishment payment. Garnishments are used for debts such as unpaid taxes, monetary fines, child support payments and defaulted student loans. *(For a debtor's wage to be garnished, a creditor must typically obtain a court order by saying that the debtor owes money and they have defaulted on payment.)*

GENERAL LEDGER   A general ledger is a company's set of numbered accounts for its accounting records. The ledger provides a complete record of financial transactions over the life of the company. The ledger holds account information that is needed to prepare financial statements and includes accounts for assets, liabilities, owners' equity, revenues and expenses.

GOOD FAITH ESTIMATE   An estimate of the fees due at closing for a mortgage loan that must be provided by a lender to a borrower within three days of the lender taking a borrower's loan application. A good faith estimate is required by the Real Estate Settlement Procedures Act (RESPA). This information is listed on a

HUD-1 form. While the form of the estimate is standardized across the industry to allow borrowers to compare costs between lenders, it is key to note that it is only an estimate, and the true figure can sometimes be different.

(Consumers should beware of unscrupulous lenders who add their own "junk" fees and/or charge excessive fees for items such as wire transfers.)

GROSS INCOME   Gross income, or gross pay, is an individual's total pay before accounting for taxes or other deductions. At the company level, it's the company's revenue minus the cost of good sold. In this case it is also referred to as gross profit and, when expressed as a percentage of revenue, gross margin. *(Gross income is an individual's income and receipts from nearly all sources. Sources of gross income or pay include salary, wages, tips, capital gains, dividends, interest, rents, pensions and alimony.)*

GUARANTOR   A guarantor is a person who guarantees to pay for someone else's debt if he or she should default on a loan obligation. A guarantor acts as a co-signer of sorts, in that they pledge their own assets or services if a situation arises in which the original debtor cannot perform their obligations. Also known as a Surety.

H

HEAD OF HOUSEHOLD   A status held by the person in a household who is running the household and looking after a qualified dependent. In order to qualify as head of household, the designated household must be located at the person's home and the person must pay more than 50% of the costs involved in running the household. The benefit of having the head-of-household status is that it can result in lower tax rates in certain jurisdictions.

Health Maintenance Organization – HMO   A health maintenance organization (HMO) is an organization that provides health coverage for a monthly or annual fee. A Health Maintenance Organization (HMO) is a group of medical insurance providers that limit coverage to medical aid provided from doctors that are under the contract of HMO. These contracts allow for premiums to be lower since the health providers have the advantage of having patients directed to them; but these contracts also add additional restrictions to HMO's members.

Health Reimbursement Account – HRA   An HRA, or health reimbursement account, consists of employer-funded plans that reimburse employees for incurred medical expenses that are not covered by the company's standard insurance plan. Because the employer funds the plan, any distributions are considered tax deductible to the employer. Reimbursement dollars received by the employee are generally tax free. A health reimbursement account is also known as a health reimbursement arrangement.

Healthcare Power Of Attorney – HCPA   A legal form that allows an individual to empower another with decisions regarding his or her healthcare and medical treatment. Healthcare power of attorney becomes active when a person is unable to make decisions or consciously communicate intentions regarding treatments.

Health Insurance Portability And Accountability Act – HIPAA An act created by the U.S Congress in 1996 that amends both the Employee Retirement Income Security Act (ERISA) and the Public Health Service Act (PHSA) in an effort to protect individuals covered by health insurance and to set standards for the storage and privacy of personal medical data.

(The HIPAA ensures that individual health care plans are accessible, portable, and renewable, and it sets the standards and the methods for how medical data is shared across the U.S. health system in order to prevent fraud. It pre-empts state law unless the state's regulations are more stringent.)

Health Savings Account – HSA   A Health Savings Account (HSA) is a tax-advantaged account created for individuals who are covered under high-deductible health plans (HDHPs) to save for medical expenses that HDHPs do not cover. Contributions are made into the account by the individual or the individual's employer and are limited to a maximum amount each year. The contributions are invested over time and can be used to pay for qualified medical expenses, which include most medical care such as dental, vision and over-the-counter drugs.

Home Affordable Refinance Program (HARP)   A mortgage-refinancing program offered by the Federal Housing Finance Agency to homeowners who own homes that are worth less than the outstanding balance on the loan. Homeowners eligible for Home Affordable Refinance Program (HARP) loans have mortgages owned or guaranteed by either Freddie Mac or Fannie Mae that were sold to either Fannie or Freddie before May 31, 2009.

Homeowner's Association – HOA   A homeowner's association (HOA) is an organization in a subdivision, planned community or condominium that makes and enforces rules for the properties within its jurisdiction. Those who purchase property within an HOA's jurisdiction automatically become members and are required to pay dues, known as HOA fees. Some associations can be very restrictive about what members can do with their properties.

HOMESTEAD EXEMPTION   A homestead exemption protects the value of a home from property taxes and creditors following the death of a homeowner spouse. A homestead exemption can be found in state statutes and constitutional provisions across the U.S. and is an automatic benefit in some states. In states where the homestead protection is not automatic, homeowners must file a claim which must be re-filed when moving primary residences.

HOME WARRANTY   A residential service contract undertaken by a home owner that covers the cost of maintaining household systems or appliances. A home warranty provides coverage for a set period-of-time and varies from state to state and company to company. A home warranty is not the same thing as a home insurance. *(When an individual purchases a home, s/he may not be privy to how well the previous owners maintained and managed the components of the home. For this reason home buyers are usually encouraged to purchase a home warranty. It will help reduce the high* *costs associated with paying for damages or replacements on multiple components of the home.)*

I

IN ESCROW   In escrow is an item such as money or a piece of property that has been transferred to a third party with the intentions of delivery to a grantee as part of a binding agreement. Valuables in escrow are delivered, generally by an escrow agent, to a grantee upon satisfaction of outlined terms. *(Escrowed items are most commonly found in real estate transactions. Property, cash and the title to the property are often held in escrow until all specified conditions are met, and transfer of ownership can occur.)*

INSUFFICIENT FUNDS   Insufficient funds is an issue that occurs when an account does not have adequate capital to satisfy a payment demand. Insufficient funds in an account may also be referred to as "non-sufficient funds" or "NSF."

INTEREST ONLY MORTGAGE   An interest-only mortgage is a type of mortgage in which the mortgagor is required to pay only interest with the principal repaid in a lump sum at a specified date.

IRA ROLLOVER   An Individual Retirement Arrangement (IRA) rollover is a transfer of funds from a retirement account into a traditional IRA or a Roth IRA. This can occur either through a direct transfer or by a check, which the custodian of the distributing account writes to the account holder who then deposits it into another IRA account.

(IRA rollovers can occur from a retirement account such as a 401(k) into an IRA, or as an IRA to IRA transfer. Most rollovers occur when people change jobs and wish to move 401(k) or 403(b) assets into an IRA, but some occur when account holders simply want to switch to an IRA with better benefits or investment choices.)

IRA PLAN   A plan that individuals may establish to arrange and plan for retirement. Generally, an IRA plan allows you to save money and defer taxes until you retire. IRA plans have annual contribution limits that are established by the government and rise gradually with inflation; individuals age 50 and older can make slightly higher "catch-up" contributions. *(Individual retirement account plans come in several forms: the traditional IRA and the Roth IRA for individuals, and the SEP IRA and the SIMPLE IRA for the self-employed (self-employed individuals may still use traditional or Roth IRAs). Each plan has different rules regarding taxation and withdrawals. The tax advantages of these types of accounts make them valuable as retirement savings tools.)*

L

LAND CONTRACT   An agreement between a buyer and seller of property in which the buyer makes payments toward full ownership (as with a mortgage), but in a land contract, the title or deed is held by the owner until the full payment is made. This type of contract is technically not a legally binding agreement and, therefore, many different types of payment formats can be found. As in a standard mortgage, there is an agreed upon price and payment schedule, but the payments are often not amortized evenly, so that a large balloon payment may be required to complete the purchase. *(A land contract can be thought of as a "lease with an option to buy".)*

LAST WILL and TESTAMENT   A last will and testament is a legal document that communicates a person's final wishes pertaining to possessions and dependents. A person's last will and testament outlines what to do with possessions, whether he is leaving them to another person or group or donating them to charity, and what happens to other things for which he is responsible, such as custody of dependents and accounts and interests management.

LEASE OPTION   An agreement that gives a renter the choice to purchase a property during or at the end of the rental period. As long as the lease option period is in effect, the landlord/seller may not offer the property for sale to anyone else. When the term expires, the renter must either exercise or forfeit the purchase option. A lease option gives a renter/potential buyer more flexibility than a lease-purchase agreement, which requires the renter to purchase the property at the end of the rental period.

LEMON LAWS   Lemon laws are regulations that attempt to protect consumers in the event that they purchase a defective vehicle or other consumer products or services, referred to as lemons, that does not meet their purported quality or usefulness. Lemon laws apply to defects that affect the use, safety or value of a vehicle or product. If the product cannot be repaired successfully after a reasonable number of attempts, the manufacturer must repurchase or replace it. *(Lemon laws vary by state. These laws often cover new vehicle purchases, but can be applied towards other purchases or leases.)*

LIFE ANNUITY   An insurance product that features a predetermined periodic payout amount until the death of the annuitant. These products are most frequently used to help retirees budget their money after retirement. Typically, the annuitant pays into the annuity on a periodic basis when he or she is still working. However, annuitants may also buy the annuity product in one large purchase. When the annuitant retires, the annuity makes periodic (usually monthly) payouts to the annuitant, providing a reliable source of income. When a triggering event (such as death) occurs, the periodic payments from the annuity usually cease.

LIMITED LIABILITY COMPANY-LLC   A limited liability company (LLC) is a corporate structure whereby the members of the company cannot be held personally liable for the company's debts or liabilities. Limited liability companies are essentially hybrid entities that combine the characteristics of a corporation and a partnership or sole proprietorship. While the limited liability feature is similar to that of a corporation, the availability of flow-through taxation to the members of an LLC is a feature of partnerships. *(Although LLCs have some attractive features, they also have a number of disadvantages, especially in relation to the structure of a corporation. A LLC has to be dissolved upon the death or bankruptcy of a member, unlike a corporation, which can exist in perpetuity.)*

LIQUIDATE Liquidate means to convert assets into cash or cash equivalents by selling them on the open market. Liquidate is also a term used in bankruptcy procedures in which an entity chooses or is forced by a legal judgment or contract to turn assets into a "liquid" form (cash). In finance, an asset is an item that has value.

M

MANDATORY DISTRIBUTION   The amount an individual must withdraw from certain types of tax-advantaged retirement accounts each year in order to avoid tax penalties. Mandatory distributions go into effect in the year an individual turns 70 ½ years old. The Internal Revenue Service's (IRS) official name for mandatory distributions is "required minimum distributions," or RMDs. Mandatory distributions apply to traditional IRAs, 401(k)s, 403(b)s, 457 (b)s, SEPs, SARSEPs, SIMPLE IRAs and Roth 401(k)s.

MANAGEMENT FEE   A management fee is a charge levied by an investment manager for managing an investment fund. The management fee is intended to compensate the managers for their time and expertise for selecting stocks and managing the portfolio. It can also include other items such as investor relations expenses and the administration costs of the fund. The management fee is the cost of having your assets professionally managed.

MARITAL PROPERTY   A U.S. state-level legal distinction of a married individual's assets. Property acquired by either spouse during the course of a marriage is considered marital property. For example, an IRA in the name of an individual with a spouse that is accumulated during the course of the marriage would be considered marital property. Also known as "community property".

MATURITY DATE   The maturity date is the date on which the principal amount of a note, draft, acceptance bond or another debt instrument becomes due and is repaid to the investor and interest payments stop. It is also the termination or due date on which an installment loan must be paid in full.

MECHANIC'S LIEN   A guarantee of payment to builders, contracters and construction firms that build or repair structures. Mechanic's liens also extend to suppliers of materials and subcontractors and cover building repairs as well. The lien ensures that the workmen are paid before anyone else in the event of liquidation.

A mechanic's lien is also known as "artisans' liens" or "materialmen's liens".

MEDICAID   Medicaid is a healthcare program that assists low-income families or individuals in paying for long-term medical and custodial care costs. Medicaid is a joint program, funded primarily by the federal government and run at the state level, where coverage may vary. Medicaid is available only to individuals and families who meet specified criteria. Recipients must be legal permanent residents or citizens of the United States and may include adults with low income, their dependents, and people with specified disabilities. *(Medicaid is a government-sponsored insurance program for individuals of any age whose resources and income are insufficient to cover healthcare.)*

MEDICAL SAVINS ACCOUNT   A medical plan combining high-deductible medical insurance protection with a tax-deferred savings account that can be offered by employers as part of a benefits package. Medical savings accounts are designed to help participants pay for medical and healthcare expenses by allowing them to save for those expenses in a tax-sheltered environment. Participants pay healthcare expenses from this account up to the amount of the insurance deductible.

Also known as "Archer medical savings accounts" or "Archer MSAs."

MEDICARE   Medicare is a U.S. federal health program that subsidizes people who meet one of the following criteria:

1 An individual aged 65 or older who has been a U.S. citizen or permanent legal resident for five years.

2 An individual who is disabled and has collected Social Security for a minimum of two years.

3 An individual who is undergoing dialysis for kidney failure or who is in need of a kidney transplant.

4 An individual who has Amyotrophic Lateral Sclerosis (Lou Gehrig's disease).

Medicare helps out people at a time in their lives when they may have serious health problems but lack the funding for treatment. *(Medicare is divided into two parts. The first part of the coverage encompasses in-patient hospital, skilled nursing facility, home health and hospice care. The second part of coverage encompasses almost all the necessary medical services (doctors' services, laboratory and x-ray services, wheelchairs, etc)*

MORTGAGE INSURANCE Mortgage insurance is an insurance policy that protects a mortgage lender or title holder in the event that the borrower defaults on payments, dies, or is otherwise unable to meet the contractual obligations of the mortgage. Mortgage insurance can refer to private mortgage insurance (PMI), mortgage life insurance, or mortgage title insurance. What these have in common is an obligation to make the lender or property holder whole in the event of specific cases of loss.

(For homeowners who are required to have PMI because of the 80 percent loan-to-value ratio rule, they can request that the insurance policy be canceled once 20 percent of the principal balance has been paid off.)

MORTGAGE MODIFICATION A permanent change in a homeowner's home loan terms that makes the monthly loan payments affordable. The goal of mortgage modification is to prevent foreclosure. Mortgage modification can benefit homeowners by preventing them from losing their home and can benefit lenders by avoiding the costly foreclosure process. *(To apply for a mortgage modification, a homeowner must complete an application package documenting income, assets, expenses and financial hardship.)*

MORTGAGE SHORT SALE The sale of a property by a financially distressed borrower for less than the outstanding mortgage balance due where the proceeds from the sale will be used to repay the lender. The lender then accepts the less-than-full repayment of the mortgage (and the borrower is released from the mortgage obligation) in order to avoid what would amount to larger losses for the lender if it were to foreclose on the mortgage.

MUTUAL FUND   A mutual fund is an investment vehicle made up of a pool of moneys collected from many investors for the purpose of investing in securities such as stocks, bonds, money market instruments and other assets. Mutual funds are operated by professional money managers, who allocate the fund's investments and attempt to produce capital gains and/or income for the fund's investors. A mutual fund's portfolio is structured and maintained to match the investment objectives stated in its prospectus.

N

NASDAQ   A global electronic marketplace for buying and selling securities, as well as the benchmark index for U.S. technology stocks. Nasdaq was created by the National Association of Securities Dealers (NASD) to enable investors to trade securities on a computerized, speedy and transparent system, and commenced operations on February 8, 1971. The term "Nasdaq" is also used to refer to the Nasdaq Composite, an index of more than 3,000 stocks listed on the Nasdaq exchange that includes the world's foremost technology and biotech giants such as Apple, Google, Microsoft, Oracle, Amazon, Intel and Amgen.

NET WORTH   Net worth is the amount by which assets exceed liabilities. Net worth is a concept applicable to individuals and businesses as a key measure of how much an entity is worth. A consistent increase in net worth indicates good financial health; conversely, net worth may be depleted by annual operating losses or a substantial decrease in asset values relative to liabilities.

O

OPERATING COST   Operating costs are expenses associated with the maintenance and administration of a business on a day-to-day basis. The operating cost is a component of operating income and is usually reflected on a company's income statement. While operating costs generally do not include capital outlays, they can include many components of operating a business including:

   1. Bank charges

2. Sales and marketing costs

3. Travel expenses

4. Entertainment costs

5. Non-capitalized research and development expenses

6. Office supply costs

7. Rent

8. Repair and maintenance costs

9. Utility expenses

10. Salary and wage expenses

11. Accounting and Legal fees

The formula for operating cost can be expressed in the following way: *Operating Cost = Cost of Goods Sold + Operating Expenses*

OPERATING INCOME   Operating income is an accounting figure that measures the amount of profit realized from a business's operations, after deducting operating expenses such as cost of goods sold (COGS), wages and depreciation. Operating income takes a company's gross income, which is equivalent to revenue minus COGS, and subtracts all operating expenses and depreciation. A business's operating expenses are costs incurred from operating activities and include items such as office supplies, heat and electricity. *(Operating income is a measurement that shows how much of a company's revenue will eventually become profit.)*

ORIGINATION FEE   An origination fee is an upfront fee charged by a lender for processing a new loan application, used as compensation for putting the loan in place. Origination fees are quoted as a percentage of the total loan and are generally between 0.5 and 1% on mortgage loans in the United States. *(An origination fee is similar to any commission-based payment.)*

P

PATENT   A patent is a government license that gives the holder exclusive rights to a process, design or new invention for a designated period of time. Applications for patents are usually handled by a government agency. In the United States, the U.S. Patent and Trademark Office handles application and documentation. (Most patents are valid for 20 years in America) SEE PROVISIONAL PATENT

PENSION PLAN   A pension plan is a retirement plan that requires an employer to make contributions into a pool of funds set aside for a worker's future benefit. The pool of funds is invested on the employee's behalf, and the earnings on the investments generate income to the worker upon retirement. A pension plan may allow a worker to contribute part of his current income from wages into an investment plan to help fund retirement.

PERSONAL PROPERTY   Personal property is a type of property which can include any asset other than real estate. The distinguishing factor between personal property and real estate is that personal property is movable; that is, the asset is not fixed permanently to one location as with real property, such as land or buildings. Examples of personal property include vehicles, furniture, boats, and collectibles.

PREPAID FINANCE CHARGE   Charges on a loan agreement which are not included as part of the principal amount being borrowed. Prepaid finance charges can include such things as administration fees, loan insurance and discount points. As these expenses are not a part of the "asking amount," they are considered to be prepaid in nature. These expenses typically must be paid by the borrower at the time of loan closing. *(Prepaid finance charges, or closing costs as they are also commonly known, are common in lending agreements, including mortgage borrowing.)*

PROFIT   Profit is a financial benefit that is realized when the amount of revenue gained from a business activity exceeds the expenses, costs and taxes needed to sustain the activity. Any profit that is gained goes to the business's owners, who may or may not decide to spend it on the business. Calculated as: Profit = Total Revenue -Total Expenses

PROFIT MARGIN   Profit margin is a profitability ratios calculated as net income divided by revenue, or net profits divided by sales. Net income or net profit may be determined by subtracting all of a company's expenses, including operating costs, material costs (including raw materials) and tax costs, from its total revenue. Profit margins are expressed as a percentage and, in effect, measure how much out of every dollar of sales a company actually keeps in earnings. A 20% profit margin, then, means the company has a net income of $0.20 for each dollar of total revenue earned.

PROMISSORY NOTE   A promissory note is a financial instrument that contains a written promise by one party (the note's issuer or maker) to pay another party (the note's payee) a definite sum of money, either on demand or at a specified future date. A promissory note typically contains all the terms pertaining to the indebtedness, such as the principal amount, interest rate, maturity date, date and place of issuance, and issuer's signature. An individual or a company willing to carry the note (and provide the financing) under the agreed-upon terms. In effect, anyone becomes a lender when he issues a promissory note.

PROPRIETARY REVERSE MORTGAGE   A loan that lets senior homeowners retrieve the equity in their homes through a private company. Proprietary reverse mortgages are not widely available and make up a small percentage of the reverse mortgage market. Home equity conversion mortgages (HECMs), which are insured and tightly regulated by the federal government, make up the bulk of the reverse mortgage market.

PROVISIONAL PATENT APPLICATION   A short-term means of protecting an invention that requires less effort and expense than obtaining a formal patent. Filing a provisional patent application with the United States Patent and Trademark Office (USPTO) enables independent inventors to put a "patent pending" label on their idea for up to 12 months. This allows them to safeguard their intellectual property while they pitch their idea to manufacturers or buy time while they refine their product. *(Compared to a traditional patent, provisional patent applications (PPAs) are simpler and more concise – frequently taking less than 10 pages. In the application, the filer explains the product's design and the purpose that it serves.)*

Q

QUITCLAIM DEED   A quitclaim deed releases a person's interest in a property without stating the nature of the person's interest or rights, and with no warranties of that person's interest or rights in the property. A quitclaim deed neither states nor guarantees that the person relinquishing their claim to the property had valid ownership, but it does prevent that person (the grantor) from later claiming he/she has an interest in the property. A quitclaim deed usually includes a legal description of the property, the name of the person who is transferring his/her interest, the name of the person who is receiving that interest (the grantee), the date and both parties' notarized signatures. (Quitclaim deeds are typically used to transfer property in non-sale situations, such as transfers of property between family members.)

R

REAL ESTATE OWNED – "REO"   Real estate owned, or REO, is the name given to foreclosed-upon real estate, such as detached houses, condominiums, townhomes and land, in a lender's portfolio. Such properties end up in lender portfolios after unsuccessful sales at foreclosure auctions. A lender — often a bank or quasi-governmental entity such as Fannie Mae or Freddie Mac — takes ownership of a foreclosed property when no bidder offers the amount it seeks to cover the loan. *(When a borrower defaults on his mortgage, the pre-foreclosure period often involves either a real estate short sale or a public auction.)*

REDLINING   Redlining is an unethical practice that puts services (financial and otherwise) out of reach for residents of certain areas based on race or ethnicity. It can be seen in the systematic denial of mortgages, insurance, loans and other financial services based on location (and that area's default history) rather than an individual's qualifications and creditworthiness. Notably, the policy of redlining is felt the most by residents of minority neighborhoods.

RESIDUAL INCOME   Residual income is the amount of income that an individual has after all personal debts and expenses, including a mortgage, have been paid. This calculation is usually made on a monthly basis, after the monthly debts are paid.

REVERSE MORTGAGE   A reverse mortgage is a type of mortgage in which a homeowner can borrow money against the value of his or her home, receiving funds in the form of a fixed monthly payment or a line of credit. No repayment of the mortgage (principal or interest), is required until the borrower dies, moves away permanently or sells the home. The transaction is structured so that the loan amount will not exceed the value of the home over the life of the loan.

REVOLVING ACCOUNT   A type of credit account in which the customer may defer payment on part of the balance. Interest is charged on the unpaid balance and added to the total owed. A credit card is one type of revolving account. A revolving account may also be called a "line of credit" or "credit line".

RIGHT OF FIRST REFUSAL   A right of first refusal is a contractual right of an entity to be given the opportunity to enter into a business transaction with a person or company before anyone else can. If the entity with the right of first refusal declines to enter into a transaction, the owner of the asset is free to open the bidding up to other interested parties.

ROTH IRA   Named for Delaware Senator William Roth and established by the Taxpayer Relief Act of 1997, a Roth IRA is an individual retirement plan (a type of qualified retirement plan) that bears many similarities to the traditional IRA. The biggest distinction between the two is how they're taxed. *(Traditional IRA contributions are generally made with pretax dollars; you pay income tax when you withdraw the money from the account during retirement. Conversely, Roth IRAs are funded with after-tax dollars; the contributions are not tax deductible (although you may be able to take a tax credit of 10to 50% of the contribution), depending on your income and life situation). But when you start withdrawing funds, qualified distributions (see below) are tax free.)*

RULE 72(t)   Rule 72(t), issued by the Internal Revenue Service (IRS), permits penalty-free withdrawals from IRA accounts and other tax-advantaged retirement accounts like 401 (k) and 403 (b) plans. There are provisions to the rule: the owner takes at least five substantially equal periodic payments (SEPPs), with the amount depending on the owner's life expectancy as calculated through IRS-approved methods.

This rule also permits account holders to benefit from their retirement savings before retirement age, through early withdrawal, without the otherwise required 10% penalty. The withdrawals are still taxed at the owner's normal income tax rate.

SANDWICH LEASE   A lease in which a party rents property from the property owner and then subsequently leases it out to another tenant. In a sandwich lease, the primary party is both a lessee and a lessor, meaning that the party both collects rent and pays rent. Not all property owners allow this sort of arrangement. *(A sandwich lease involves a party sub-letting what is already being sub-let.)*

SELF-EMPLOYMENT TAX   Money that a small business owner must pay to the federal government to fund Medicare and Social Security. Self-employment tax is due when an individual has net earnings of $400 or more in self-employment income over the course of the tax year. In any business, both the company and the employee are taxed to pay for these two major social welfare programs. When an individual is self-employed, she is both the company and the employee, so she pays both shares of this tax. Self-employment tax is computed and reported on IRS Form 1040, Schedule SE. *(Individuals typically pay self-employment tax on 92.35% of their net earnings, not 100%. Self-employment tax is also a tax-deductible expense.)*

SETTLEMENT STATEMENT   A statement that summarizes all the fees and charges that both the homebuyer and seller face during the settlement process of a housing transaction. This form, which is under the jurisdiction of the U.S. Department of Housing and Urban Development, is also known as the HUD-1.

SHERIFF'S SALE   A sheriff's sale is a public auction where mortgage lenders, banks, tax collectors, and other litigants can collect money lost on property. A sheriff sale occurs at the end of the foreclosure process when the initial property owner can no longer make good on his or her mortgage payments. A sheriff sale can also occur to satisfy judgment and tax liens.

SHORT SALE   A short sale is a transaction in which an investor sells borrowed securities in anticipation of a price decline and is required to return an equal number of shares at some point in the future. A short seller makes money if the stock goes down in price, while a long position makes money when the stock goes up. In real estate, a short sale means selling a house for less than the mortgage owed with the lender's approval.

SIMPLE IRA   A SIMPLE IRA is a retirement savings plan that can be used by most small businesses with 100 or fewer employees. "SIMPLE" stands for "Savings Investment Match Plan for Employees." "IRA" stands for "individual retirement account." Employers can choose to make a mandatory 2% retirement account contribution to all employees or an optional matching contribution of up to 3%. Employees can contribute a maximum of $12,500 annually in 2018; the maximum is increased periodically to account for inflation. Retirement savers age 50 and older may make an additional catch-up contribution of $3,000 bringing their annual maximum to $15,500.

SOLE PROPRIETORSHIP   A sole proprietorship, also known as a sole trader or a proprietorship, is an unincorporated business with a single owner who pays personal income tax on profits earned from the business. With little government regulation, a sole proprietorship is the simplest business to set up or take apart, making sole proprietorships popular among individual self-contractors, consultants or small business owners. Many sole proprietors do business under their own names because creating a separate business or trade name isn't necessary.

STOCK   Stock is a type of security that signifies ownership in a corporation and represents a claim on part of the corporation's assets and earnings. There are two main types of stock: common and preferred. Common stock usually entitles the owner to vote at shareholders' meetings and to receive dividends. Preferred stock generally does not have voting rights, but has a higher claim on assets and earnings than the common shares. For example, owners of preferred stock receive dividends before common shareholders and have priority in the event that a company goes bankrupt and is liquidated. Also known as "shares" or "equity."

STOCK ANALYSIS   Stock analysis is the evaluation of a particular trading instrument, an investment sector, or the market as a whole. Stock analysts attempt to determine the future activity of an instrument, sector, or market. (There are two basic types of stock analysis: fundamental analysis and technical analysis:

> - Fundamental analysis concentrates on data from sources including financial records, economic reports, company assets, and market share.

> ♦ Technical analysis focuses on the study of past market action to predict future price movement.

STATE MEDICAID   Health initiatives managed by state governments in conjunction with the federal Medicaid program that help qualified low-income individuals and families pay for the costs associated with healthcare. State Medicaid programs use federal funding along with their own state funding to provide needed health services for eligible individuals, where eligibility is based on numerous factors, including income, assets, age, disability and citizenship.

SUBPRIME LENDER   A type of lender that specializes in lending to borrowers with a tainted or limited credit history. Subprime lending is more concentrated in a smaller number of large lenders than prime lending. The subprime loan market is more tiered compared to the prime loan market, where terms and rates vary little between borrowers.

T

TAX ADVISOR   A financial expert with advanced training and knowledge of tax law. The services of a tax advisor are usually retained in order to minimize taxation while remaining compliant with the law in complicated financial situations. Tax advisors can include Certified Public Accounts, tax attorneys and financial advisors. (GET ONE)

TAX AVOIDANCE   Tax avoidance is the use of legal methods to modify an individual's financial situation to lower the amount of income tax owed. This is generally accomplished by claiming the permissible deductions and credits. This practice differs from tax evasion, which uses illegal methods, such as underreporting income to avoid paying taxes. *(Tax avoidance is built into the Internal Revenue Code (IRC), which spans more than 75,000 pages. Lawmakers have used the IRC to manipulate taxpayer behavior by offering tax credits, deductions and exemptions in various aspects of people's lives including health care, saving and investing, education, energy use and other activities.)*

TAX EXEMPT   Tax exempt refers to income earnings or transactions that are free from tax at the federal, state or local level. When a taxpayer earns wages or sells an asset for a gain, that individual is creating a tax liability. While a tax deduction refers to an amount that reduces a tax liability, a tax-exempt item is excluded from any tax calculations. (One common type of tax-exempt income is interest earned on municipal bonds, which are bonds issued by states and cities to raise funds for general operations or for a specific project. When a taxpayer earns interest income on municipal bonds issued in his state of residence, the income is exempt from both federal and state taxes. Be sure to consult a tax professional.)

TITLE   A title is a legal document that espouses an individual's right to ownership and possession of all items that can be recognized as being owned or belonging to a person or a thing. At a basic level, a title is a document that indicates recognition of ownership. In a government system that acknowledges individual property rights, an individual is capable of having ownership over an expansive amount of tangible and intangible property. Titles can be obtained by purchase, descent or grant. (While there are various types of titles, there are two which are most commonly obtained: personal property titles and real property titles.)

TITLE INSURANCE   Title insurance is indemnity insurance that protects the holder from financial loss sustained from defects in a title to a property. The most common type of title insurance is lender's title insurance, which the borrower purchases only to protect the lender. Owner's title insurance, paid for by the seller to protect the buyer's equity in the property, is available separately. *(Title insurance protects both real estate owners and lenders against loss or damage occurring from liens, encumbrances, or defects in the title, or actual ownership of, a property.)*

TITLE SEARCH   An examination of public records to determine and confirm a property's legal ownership, and find out what claims are on the property. A title search is usually performed by a title company or an attorney, who researches the vested owner, the liens or other judgments on the property, the loans on the property and the property taxes due. *(Before you close a deal on the purchase of a home, a title company will search public records on the property's ownership. Once the search is finished, you'll receive a preliminary title report. If there are any issues or problems with the title, you can point them out to the seller.)*

TRADITIONAL IRA   A traditional individual retirement account (IRA) allows individuals to direct pretax income towards investments that can grow tax-deferred; no capital gains or dividend income is taxed until it is withdrawn. Individual taxpayers can contribute 100% of any earned compensation up to a specified maximum dollar amount. Contributions to a traditional IRA may be tax-deductible depending on the taxpayer's income, tax-filing status and other factors.

TRIPLE NET LEASE   A triple net lease is a lease agreement that designates the lessee, which is the tenant, as being solely responsible for all the costs relating to the asset being leased, in addition to the rent fee applied under the lease. The structure of this type of lease requires the lessee to pay the net amount for three types of costs, including net real estate taxes on the leased asset, net building insurance and net common area maintenance. This type of lease can also be referred to as a net-net-net (NNN) lease.

TSA PreCHECK   TSA PreCheck is a U.S. government program that allows travelers deemed low-risk by the Transportation Security Administration (TSA) to pass through an expedited security screening at certain U.S. airports. Qualifying travelers don't have to remove their belts, shoes or lightweight jackets. They may also leave a laptop in its case and a 3-1-1 compliant bag (which can contain items with small quantities of liquids, gels, etc. such as a travel-size bottle of mouthwash) in their carry-on.

TRUST FUND   A trust fund is a fund comprised of a variety of assets intended to provide benefits to an individual or organization. A grantor establishes a trust fund to provide financial security to an individual, most often a child or grandchild, or organizations, such as a charity or other nonprofit organization. *(A trust fund can contain cash, stocks, bonds, property or other types of financial products. The recipient of a trust fund must typically wait until a certain age, or until a specified event occurs, to receive a yearly income from the fund.)*

U

U.S. SAVINGS BOND   A U.S. savings bond is a government bond that offers a fixed rate of interest over a fixed period of time. Many people find these bonds attractive because they are not subject to state or local income taxes. These bonds cannot easily be transferred and are non-negotiable. *(A U.S. savings bond is a common type of government bond, which is a bond issued by a governmental body to raise funds from the public to fund its capital projects and other operations necessary to manage the economy.)*

UMBRELLA INSURANCE POLICY   A type of insurance policy that provides excess coverage above and beyond the liability coverage amounts in a standard insurance policy. The umbrella policy provides extra protection in the event that a lawsuit exceeds the basic level of coverage in the standard policy. *(An umbrella personal liability policy extends the basic coverage provided in different types of liability coverage, including home, auto, boat and tenant policies. This type of policy provides broad coverage, meaning that some claims that would not be covered by a standard policy may be covered under the umbrella policy.)*

UNDERWATER MORTGAGE   An underwater mortgage is a home purchase loan with a higher principal than the free-market value of the home. This situation can occur when property values are falling. In an underwater mortgage the homeowner may not have any equity available for credit. An underwater mortgage can potentially prevent a borrower from refinancing or selling the home unless they have cash to pay the loss out of pocket.

UNDERWRITING FEES   Underwriting fees are monies collected by underwriters for performing underwriting services. Underwriters work in a variety of markets including investments, mortgages and insurance. In each situation, the underwriter's jobs vary slightly yet each collects underwriting fees in exchange for his or her underwriting services. *(In capital markets, underwriting fees are collected by underwriters who administer the issuing and distributing of certain financial instruments, such as home mortgages.)*

UNSECURED DEBT   Unsecured debt is a loan that is not backed by an underlying asset. Unsecured debt includes credit card debt, medical bills, utility bills and other types of loans or credit that were extended without a collateral requirement. This type of debt presents a high risk for lenders, also referred to as the creditor, since they may have to sue for repayment if the borrower doesn't repay the full amount owed.

UNIVERSAL LIFE INSURANCE   Universal life insurance is type of flexible permanent life insurance offering the low-cost protection of term life insurance as well as a savings element (like whole life insurance), which is invested to provide a cash value buildup. The death benefit, savings component and premiums can be reviewed and altered as a policyholder's circumstances change. Unlike whole life insurance, universal life insurance allows the policyholder to use the interest from his accumulated savings to help pay premiums over time.

UTILITY PATENT = A utility patent is a patent that covers the creation of a new or improved and useful product, process or machine. A utility patent, also known as a "patent for invention," prohibits other individuals or companies from making, using or selling the invention without authorization. When most people refer to a patent, they are most likely referring to a utility patent. *(Utility patents are very valuable assets because they give inventors exclusive commercial rights to producing and utilizing the latest technology.)*

V

VA LOAN A mortgage loan program established by the United States Department of Veterans Affairs to help veterans and their families obtain home financing. The Department of Veterans Affairs does not directly originate VA loans; instead, they establish the rules for those who may qualify, dictate the terms of the mortgages offered and insure VA loans against default. (VA loans offer up to 100% financing on the value of a home. To qualify for a VA loan, borrowers must present a certificate of eligibility, which establishes their record of military service, to the lender. VA loans, FHA loans and other loans insured by departments of the United States government are securitized by the Government National Mortgage Association (Ginnie Mae)

VALUATION Valuation is the process of determining the current worth of an asset or a company; there are many techniques used to determine value. An analyst placing a value on a company looks at the company's management, the composition of its capital structure, the prospect of future earnings and market value of assets.

VESTED BENEFIT A vested benefit is a financial incentive of employment that an employee is fully entitled to. Employers sometimes offer their employees benefits that they acquire full ownership of gradually or suddenly, as they accumulate more time with the company. This process is called graduated vesting or cliff vesting, and its purpose is to give employees a reason to stay with the company long term. When the employee has earned full rights to the incentive after a predetermined number of years of service, those benefits are called fully vested. *(An example of a type of benefit that might vest gradually is shares of the company's stock. 5 years of services is generally used for time vested.)*

W

WARRANTY DEED   A warranty deed is a document that provides the greatest amount of protection to the purchaser of property as it pledges or warrants that the owner owns the property free and clear of any outstanding liens, mortgages, or other encumbrances against it.

A general warranty deed provides the grantee with the highest form of protection as it assures the following basic warranties:

- The grantor warrants that they are the rightful owner of the property and have a legal right to transfer the title.

- The grantor warrants that the property is free and clear of all liens and that there are no outstanding claims on the property from any type of creditor using it as collateral.

- There is a guarantee that the title would withstand any third-party claims to ownership of the property.

- The grantor will do whatever is necessary to make good the grantee's title to the property

WAGE EARNER PLAN (CHAPTER 13 BANKRUPTCY)
Also known as a Chapter 13 bankruptcy, this enables individuals with regular income to develop a plan to repay all or part of their debts for a period of three to five years. The repayment period depends on the debtor's monthly income as compared to the applicable state median. During this repayment period, the law forbids creditors from starting or continuing collection efforts. Chapter 13 was formerly called a wage earner's plan because relief under it was only available to individuals who earned a regular wage. Subsequent statute changes expanded it to include any individual, including the self-employed and those operating an unincorporated business.

WHOLE LIFE INSURANCE POLICY   Whole life insurance is a contract with premiums that includes insurance and investment components. The insurance component pays a predetermined amount when the insured individual dies. The investment component builds an accumulated cash value the insured individual can borrow against or withdraw. This is the most basic type of cash-value life insurance.

WILL   A will, also known as a Last Will and Testament, is a legally enforceable declaration of how a person wants his property or assets to be distributed after death. In a will, a person can also recommend a guardian for his minor children and make provisions for any surviving pets.

(Making a will is a very important component of estate planning. In it, the writer expresses his decisions about who gets his belongings and assets when he dies. If an individual dies without leaving a will, the distribution of his property is left up to the government, and may even end up becoming state property. A will ensures that the person's wishes are carried out, and it can make things easier for his heirs.)

Get *"Living Your Best Life **Workbook**"* for all forms and lists. Continue your quest to financial control!!!

SOLD SEPERATELY

To share your story of how this material has helped you, your family or friends or if you are interested in booking D Wayne, Please Email D Wayne at:

doingmybestlife@gmail.com